And You Visited Me:

Sacramental Ministry to the Sick and the Dying

*Studies in the Reformed Rites
of the Catholic Church,
Volume VI*

Charles W. Gusmer

And You Visited Me:

Sacramental Ministry to the Sick and the Dying

Pueblo Publishing Company

New York

Design: Frank Kacmarcik

Scriptural pericopes quoted from the Revised Standard
Version.

Excerpts from the English Translation of *Pastoral Care of the
Sick: Rites of Anointing and Viaticum* © 1982, International
Committee on English in the Liturgy, Inc. All rights reserved.

ISBN: 0–916134–61–X

Printed in the United States of America.

For My Students
At Darlington,
St. Michael's College,
Notre Dame,
And Collegeville

Christ, medicine of the heavenly Father
and truest doctor of the human family's health,
to the humble prayer of thy provident people
    in thy power grant favor.

Lo, we beseech thee on behalf of the sick,
who shiver with dreaded attacks of the plague
that in thy mercy thou wilt lift from the ailing
    the sickness that shakes them.

Thou who showedst forth thy power
and straightway healedst Peter's wife's mother,
and likewise the son of the royal official
    and the centurion's servant,

Heal the diseases of body and soul:
apply thy cure to the causes of our wounds,
lest without profit the tormenting plague
    burn our bodies.

Do thou bring vigor to thy weakened flock,
Pour forth abundance of health on thy people,
restoring the sick to their former health
    as thou art wont.

Let all hostile attacks fall back,
and every onslaught of pain melt away;
let strength and health returning soothe
    the limbs of the grieving.

Lord, take pity on our lamentation
now, as we beseech thee to cure us,
that every sufferer yet on his sickbed
    may be touched by thy healing.

'Though now beset by present ills,
then in company fit knowing God's will,
may they, enjoying fruitful unity,
    enter heaven's kingdom.

Christe, caelestis medicina Patris,
hymn from the Mozarabic Office for the Sick (*7th century*)

Contents

Introduction

The Latin typical edition of the *Rite of Anointing and Pastoral Care of the Sick* was released by the Roman Congregation for Worship on December 7, 1972. From 1973 to 1983 the English-speaking dioceses of the Roman Catholic Communion used a provisional text, the so-called Green Book of the International Committee on English in the Liturgy (ICEL).

At the time, the immediate concern was to make available a translation from the Latin typical edition which on the basis of pastoral experience could be improved upon later in the more definitive White Book. In December 1975, the U.S. Bishops' Committee on the Liturgy asked for a broad-based consultation from all who had used the interim rite, especially priests and hospital chaplains. The BCL *Newsletter* suggested the following areas for the consultation:

1. the translation of the text;
2. the layout and presentation of the rite;
3. the selection and position of the scripture readings;
4. the use and presentation of options;
5. the use and adequacy of individual rubrics;
6. suggested additions to the rite or its general introduction;
7. suggested adaptations for the dioceses of the United States;
8. suggestions as to how the rite might be made more pastorally useful.

Basing their work as far as possible on the responses received, the ICEL committees for the Presentation of

Texts and the Translation and Revision of Original Texts began preparing the final textual version, or White Book, in 1977. The published result of their labors is entitled *Pastoral Care of the Sick: Rites of Anointing and Viaticum*. It is this version for which this book serves as a background study and commentary.

What is new? What has been altered or added? The overall norm for this recent revision is pastoral usefulness. This has been achieved by (1) a structural reordering of rites, (2) more extended pastoral introduction, (3) helpful materials borrowed from other rituals, and (4) newly composed texts.

STRUCTURAL REORDERING OF RITES
Number 38 of the anointing ritual speaks of adaptations belonging to the conferences of bishops. One of these is "to arrange the material in the editions of liturgical books prepared under the direction of the conferences of bishops in a format that will be as suitable as possible for pastoral use." Accordingly, there is now a more clear-cut distinction between *Pastoral Care of the Sick* (Part I) and *Pastoral Care of the Dying* (Part II). Part I is comprised of Visits to the Sick (chap. 1), Visits to a Sick Child (chap. 2), Communion of the Sick (chap. 3), and Anointing of the Sick (chap. 4). Part II embraces Celebration of Viaticum (chap. 5), Commendation of the Dying (chap. 6), Prayers for the Dead (chap. 7), and Rites for Exceptional Circumstances (chap. 8).

A further rearrangement of rites is made in the distinction between the ordinary or normal celebration and the pastoral adaptation necessitated by the vicissitudes of the ministry to the sick and the dying. The ordinary or normative rite is that which is celebrated in its full form with the sick or dying person(s) and a community of Christian believers; at times, however, pastoral need or discretion may suggest something less than this. For example, chapter 3 contains a rite for Communion in Ordinary Circumstances and one for Communion in a Hospital or Institution. The ordinary rite is the fuller and more preferable celebration; the rite for hospitals and institutions recognizes the difficulty in bringing the sick together in one place and makes the appropriate adaptations. Again, chapter 4 specifies three manners of anointing the sick: Anointing outside Mass, the more usual celebration; Anointing within Mass; and a more abbreviated Anointing in a Hospital or Institution. The same principle of distinguishing between the ideal or normative and its pastoral adaptation is maintained in *Pastoral Care of the Dying*. Chapters 5, 6, and 7—Celebration of Viaticum, Commendation of the Dying, and Prayers for the Dead—are the preferred rites to be used whenever possible; chapter 8, as the title indicates, is reserved for exceptional circumstances when time is at a premium: Continuous Rite, Rite for Emergencies, and Christian Initiation for the Dying.

Each of these rites is spelled out in fuller detail and with fewer cross-references than was the case in the 1973 provisional text. A further helpful aid, already implemented in the revised *Rite of Penance* and now introduced here, is an outline of each rite's structure reproduced on a separate page before every liturgy.

PASTORAL INTRODUCTIONS
The pastoral introductions, inspired by the French ritual, are expanded and adapted from the *praenotanda* of the Roman typical edition. For material picked up from the typical edition, the original numbers appear on the right-hand margin of the book; material without such numbers is new. A considerable retranslation of the original texts has also been made to improve upon style and to achieve a language more inclusive of both sexes. Three instances of such enrichment stand out.

First, number 8 speaks of the subject of anointing as one of the faithful "whose health is seriously impaired by sickness or old age." Compare this with the previous "dangerously ill due to sickness or old age." For a long time it has troubled this writer to speak of old age as a condition of sickness; "impaired" is a far better rendering. The retranslation of *periculose aegrotans* from "dangerously" to "seriously" ill is an even greater breakthrough. The English-speaking Church owes ICEL a debt of gratitude for their forthrightness in pursuing this modification during the two years that this revision lay on the desk of the Congregation for Sacraments and Divine Worship in Rome.

A second significant change is the direct mention of the provision for anointing those wracked with mental or emotional disorders, a possibility only alluded to in the 1973 ritual:

"Some types of mental sickness are now classified as serious. Those who are judged to have a serious mental illness and who would be strengthened by the sacrament may be anointed. . . . The anointing may be repeated in accordance with the conditions for other kinds of serious illness" (no. 53).

The new and moving paragraphs on the care of a dying child, something previously quite unattended to in our liturgical books, are a further instance of pastoral enrichment.

MATERIALS FROM OTHER RITUALS
In order to make this a complete ritual book in ministering to all the sacramental needs of the sick and dying, it was necessary to include materials found in other already existing rituals.

A pastor once told me that in responding to sick calls

he always brought both the *Rite of Anointing* and the *Rite of Funerals* with him. All too often the parishioner had already died and the prayers from chapter 1 of the funeral rite were more appropriate to console the grieving family. What he experienced in his pastoral ministry is now remedied in the present ICEL revision, where the commendation of the dying has been strengthened by including Prayers after Death and Prayers for the Family and Friends, both taken from the *Rite of Funerals*. Also from the same ritual is the new chapter 7, Prayers for the Dead, which is a liturgical ministration to comfort the survivors when the rite of anointing would not be appropriate. Prayers for the Dead concludes with the symbolic gesture of sprinkling the body with holy water, signing the forehead with the sign of the cross, or giving a simple blessing. The comprehensiveness of *Pastoral Care of the Sick* is further enhanced through the inclusion of chapter 3 of the RCIA (Short Rite of Adult Initiation in Proximate Danger of Death or at the Point of Death), which has become here Christian Initiation for the Dying. Finally, the first chapter from the *Rite of Penance*, Rite for Reconciliation of Individual Penitents, is reprinted as an appendix.

NEWLY COMPOSED TEXTS

Almost every chapter contains newly composed texts, be these antiphons for sprinkling with holy water, introductions to the penitential rite or Lord's Prayer, showing of the eucharistic bread (chap. 3, Communion of the Sick); or greetings and introductions to the Lord's Prayer (chap. 7, Prayers for the Dead). The most important additions pertain to Visits to the Sick, Visits to a Sick Child, and Anointing of the Sick. Visits to the Sick (chap. 1) is now cast more in the format of a liturgical service, similar to the structure found in the earlier Roman Ritual: reading, response, Lord's Prayer, concluding prayer, and blessing. Visits to a Sick Child

(chap. 2) is totally new and meets an important
pastoral need by employing language and gestures
readily comprehensible to the young. Anointing of the
Sick (chap. 4) begins with an introduction that has
been reworded, so as not to be so pointedly
inappropriate in terminal cases as was the provisional
text. The same pastoral sensitivity and the overall felt
need for a greater warmth of expression has also led to
newly composed prayers: "General" (perhaps more
terminal cases), "Before surgery," "For a child," "For a
young person." The "Reception of the Sick" for the
Anointing within Mass spells out more clearly the
intent of the celebration as a service of communal
anointing. Perhaps most important of all, orations and
a preface for the eucharistic prayer are now provided
for anointings within Mass.

ACKNOWLEDGMENTS
This book has been many years in process. Abbot
Laurentius Klein, O.S.B., first interested me in the rites
for the sick practiced in the Church of England, an idea
that grew into a doctoral dissertation under Professor
Dr. Balthasar Fischer at the Theological Faculty of Trier
in Germany and a subsequent publication by the
Alcuin Club in London. This book is the fruit of
courses on the rites for the sick and dying taught at
Immaculate Conception Seminary, Darlington, as well
as at summer sessions of the University of Notre Dame
and St. John's University, Collegeville. It is intended to
further the Church's ministry to the sick and dying and
to introduce the present ICEL revision.

The first chapter traces the tradition of anointing the
sick from the New Testament until the recent reform.
Chapter 2 examines the rites for the sick and is a
commentary on Part I, *Pastoral Care of the Sick*. Chapter
3 explores the rites for the dying and is a commentary
on Part II, *Pastoral Care of the Dying*. The present and

future constitute the purview of the last two chapters: chapter 4 is an attempt to synthesize the theological dimensions of sickness and healing; chapter 5 is concerned with the pastoral praxis.

The support and encouragement of many people accompany an undertaking such as this. I am grateful to the Darlington faculty, in particular to its rector/ president, the Reverend Monsignor Edward J. Ciuba, and academic dean, the Reverend Francis A. DeDomenico. Special thanks also to Jeremy Noble and James Conley for translating the Mozarabic hymn. A debt of gratitude is due James Schellman of ICEL for keeping me informed on the progress of the revision. Finally, I am indebted to Father Aidan Kavanagh, O.S.B., and to Bernard Benziger for their helpful suggestions in preparing the manuscript for publication in the series, Studies in the Reformed Rites of the Catholic Church.

Charles W. Gusmer
Immaculate Conception Seminary
Darlington, New Jersey

The Tradition

Chapter One

The Tradition of Anointing the Sick with Oil

In preparing for the Second Vatican Council and the subsequent *Constitution on the Sacred Liturgy*, comparatively few preliminary suggestions were made concerning the sacrament of anointing of the sick. Now that the Acts of the Council are being published, we know the full story.[1] Of the forty-six *vota* submitted, six bishops urged a change of name from "extreme unction" to "anointing of the sick"; four sought to have the anointing precede the commendation of the dying, as had always been preserved in the East, in various religious orders such as the Cistercians, and in the recently amended German *Collectio Rituum* (1950). Five respondents felt the seriously ill were proper subjects for the anointing; four wanted more flexibility regarding the repetition of the sacrament. One votum was for empowering deacons to anoint. Most of these suggestions were incorporated into the preparatory text:

"The sacrament which is commonly called extreme unction henceforth will be called anointing of the sick, for it is not per se a sacrament of the dying but of the seriously ill. The appropriate time for receiving it is as soon as the faithful falls into a serious illness. Sacred unction can be repeated sometimes within the same illness."[2] However, on the basis of the intervention by two cardinals and six bishops during the second session of the Council, the final text read:

"'Extreme Unction,' which may also and more fittingly be called 'Anointing of the Sick,' is not a sacrament for those only who are at the point of death. Hence, as soon as anyone of the faithful begins to be in danger of death from sickness or old age, the fitting time for him to receive this sacrament has certainly already arrived."[3]

No mention was made of repeating the sacrament. This text, voted upon by the Council Fathers on October 16, 1963 (2,143 in favor, 35 opposed), became paragraph 73 of the Constitution on the Sacred Liturgy.

What is immediately apparent is a behind-the-scenes conflict concerning the meaning of the sacrament. Is it a sacrament of dying (extreme unction), or a sacrament of the sick (anointing of the sick)?

The first opinion has exerted considerable influence in this century through the publication in 1907 of a work by J. Kern, which was a revival of the scholastic tradition of the sacrament.[4] Granting the proper disposition on the part of the recipient, the sacrament of unction has the power of canceling the total debt of punishment for sin and thus preparing the soul for immediate entrance into heaven. This scholastic approach was popularized in this country particularly by F. Tecklenberg in 1916[5] and by H.A. Reinhold and the National Liturgical Week in 1941.[6] At times the sacrament was thought to be a surer way to forgiveness of sins for one lapsing into unconsciousness and therefore unable to enter into the ministration of the sacrament of penance. This understanding of unction as a sacrament of the dying, with its corresponding purpose as the "last anointing" to prepare the soul for the beatific vision, an anointing unto glory, has been especially prominent among German systematic theologians.[7]

The second viewpoint held that unction is a sacrament of healing, a sacrament of the sick; the sacrament of the dying per se is viaticum. Herein is found the original

4

tradition of anointing as demonstrated by scripture and the first 800 years of its use. For example, James 5:14–15 has to do with a sick, not a dying, Christian. Traces of the early practice were still to be found in the unction rite of the *Rituale Romanum* of 1614, still in use prior to the Second Vatican Council, where prayers for healing and recovery are juxtaposed with the medieval form for extreme unction. This more biblical and liturgical approach has been deeply rooted in French liturgical circles and in the overall pastoral practice.[8]

Number 73 thus represents a compromise between two conflicting opinions as to the essential purpose and meaning of the sacrament. The inherited name "extreme unction" is retained, although "anointing of the sick" is preferred. The danger of death from sickness or old age remained the condition for its reception, but care should be taken that the sacrament be administered at the very beginning of any such danger.

The purpose of this chapter will be to explore the anointing of the sick in the New Testament and in the tradition of the West. This will include the first 800 years, the Carolingian turning point, the teaching of the scholastic theologians, and from the Council of Trent up to the Second Vatican Council.

NEW TESTAMENT

Anointing with oil has many religious uses in the Old Testament, late Judaism, primitive Christianity, and the early Church:[9]

1. Coronation of a king (Jgs 9:8; 1 Sm 9:16, 10:1, 15:1,17, 16:3,12; 2 Sm 2:4, 3:19; 2 Kgs 9:3,6; Pss 23:5,45:8, 89:21).
2. Ordination of a priest (Ex 28:41, 29:7, 29, 30:30–33, 40:13; Lv 4:3, 6:13, 7:36, 8:12; Nm 3:3; Dn 9:25; Sir 45:15).

3. Installation of a prophet (1 Kgs 19:16; Is 61:1; Lk 4:18).
4. Consecration of objects of cult (Gn 28:18, 31:13; Ex 29:36, 30:23−29, 37:29, 40:9; Nm 7:1,10,88; Dn 9:24).
5. Care of wounds (Is 1:6; Lk 10:34; Lv 14:15−18,26−29).
6. Healing the sick.
7. Embalming the body (Mk 16:1; Lk 24:1).

These varied uses must be seen against the backdrop of olive oil as an all-purpose medium in the ancient Mediterranean world, a multileveled meaning not completely lost even today. Oil was used for cooking and eating; even today good Italian restaurants boast that they cook only with genuine imported olive oil, or "Italian butter" as they sometimes call it. Oil provided illumination for lamps; today the Eastern Orthodox rite of unction is still sometimes referred to as the Rite of the Lamp, as the oil for anointing may be taken from oil lamps hanging before icons. Oil served as a cleansing substance in bathing similar to soap today; hence the origin of the prebaptismal oil of the catechumens with its exorcistic and purgative meaning. Oil was also a cosmetic. Chrism or the Greek *myron* is a kind of sacred perfume with a rich symbolism retained in the Greek language: through chrismation we are conformed to Christ ("Anointed One") and become Christians ("anointed ones"). Oil was used as a healing medicine, as attested to in the account of the Good Samaritan (Lk 10:29−37). In short, oil together with wheat and wine were the most important agricultural products of the day, representing ancient civilization and indeed life itself. If such a corresponding all-purpose medium exists today upon which so much of life depends, it might be petroleum with its multiple uses for industry, heating, fuel for vehicles, and synthetic products.

There are two passages in the New Testament that

have to do with the religious use of oil in anointing the sick: Mark 6:13 and James 5:14–15. The passage in Mark belongs to the apostolic ministry of healing: "And Jesus went about all the cities and villages, teaching in their synagogues and preaching the gospel of the kingdom, and healing every disease and every infirmity" (Mt 9:35). Jesus entrusted this healing ministry to the Twelve: "And he called to him his twelve disciples and gave them authority over unclean spirits, to cast them out, and to heal every disease and every infirmity" (Mt. 10:1; see also Mk 6:7; Lk 9:1). Mark is unique in his mention of anointing: "And they cast out many demons, and anointed with oil many that were sick and healed them" (Mk 6:13). Mark does not explicitly relate this anointing of the sick with either Jesus' own practice or with any specific command to his disciples. In all likelihood, it was a Palestinian custom and probably associated with exorcism. Many Roman Catholic commentators have been reluctant to see the origins of the sacrament of anointing in this apostolic ministry of healing, for the principal grace of the sacrament was thought to be the spiritual cure of the sick person, not bodily healing. A notable exception was M.J. Lagrange, who felt that the rite described in Mark might well represent the "real origins of the sacrament."[10] The Council of Trent was leaning in the same direction when in 1551 it decreed: "This sacred anointing of the sick was instituted by Christ our Lord as a true and proper sacrament of the New Testament. It is alluded to indeed by Mark (6:13), but is recommended to the faithful and promulgated by James."[11]

The epistle of James is a type of paranetic literature in the New Testament, using proverbs to convey a way of life and practical wisdom pleasing to God and neighbor. Bo Reicke has referred to James 5:12–20 as a manual of discipline.[12] Beginning with verse 13, the unifying theme of prayer is applied to three existential situations of a Christian: suffering, joy, and sickness:

"Is any one among you suffering? Let him pray. Is any cheerful? Let him sing praise. Is any among you sick? Let him call for the elders of the church, and let them pray over him, anointing him with oil in the name of the Lord; and the prayer of faith will save the sick man, and the Lord will raise him up; and if he has committed sins, he will be forgiven. Therefore confess your sins to one another, and pray for one another, that you may be healed. The prayer of a righteous man has great power in its effects" (Jas 5:13–16).

Is any among you sick (asthenei): The noun *astheneia* is found in the gospels referring to sicknesses healed by Jesus. Sometimes it is used for those near death (Jn 4:46–47; 11:1,4,14; Acts 9:37), but the word per se does not necessarily imply a grave illness. How sick is the ailing Christian? Probably sick enough to be confined to bed (the presbyters are sent for), but not *in extremis*. The philology of *kamno* ("tired, sick") in verse 15 further reinforces this understanding. The nature of the sickness is probably bodily illness, but in the Jewish mind sin and sickness are closely linked. Hence the treatment of sickness in the ancient world was not merely medicinal, but often exorcistic as well. James is unaware of the distinction between sin and sickness as we know it. He is likewise unmindful of the Hellenistic distinction between body and spirit. For James, the subject of the anointing is a complete sick person, a psychosomatic unity, and the expected result is a restoration of the whole person.

Let him call for the elders (presbyteroi) of the church: The previous verse ("among you") indicates that the sick person is a member of the Christian community. The member is now instructed to summon the presbyters, men closely associated with the apostles in authority

(Acts 15:2,4,6). Presbyters were likewise appointed over missionary churches (Acts 14:23; 20:17; 1 Tm 5:17, 19; Ti 1:5). They are not, therefore, charismatic healers such as are described in 1 Corinthians 12. Nor are they simply men of advanced years. "Elder" does not necessarily refer to chronological age, but rather at the time of the letter, the word was becoming a technical term for an official position of authority in the local church. While it might be premature to project at this early date the later hierarchy of bishop, presbyter, and deacon, the presbyters of James are officeholders, officially recognized ministers, perhaps analogous to the structure of the original community at Jerusalem.[13]

And let them pray over him, anointing him with oil in the name of the Lord: Pray *over* him, not simply *for* him. James envisions the presbyters gathering around the sick person, who most likely lies prostrate before them. This graphic local sense is the reason why Origen (d. c.254), using this passage in a presumably penitential context, interpolated the words "lay hands" on him.[14] It appears that James is not intending to introduce a new procedure but presupposes its existence: a medicinal exorcistic action on behalf of the sick. What is important, however, is that in contrast to later generations, more attention is given to the prayer of faith than to the action of anointing with oil. "In the name of the Lord" implies that this is not simply a medicinal remedy. As in Mark 6:13, it symbolizes the healing presence and power of the Lord Jesus Christ.

And the prayer of faith will save (sosei) the sick man, and the Lord will raise him up (egerei): "The prayer of faith" is a further reminder that this is not a mere medicinal aid. Elsewhere in James, *sozein* (to save) means the salvation of one's soul (1:21; 2:14; 4:12; 5:20). In the gospel's "Your faith has saved you," the verb can have a double meaning—either eternal salvation or restoration to health. The present context would suggest the latter meaning. *Egerein* ("to raise up") may mean either resurrection or to be raised up from sickness, to be made whole again. In this context it is expected that the sick person will be at least "saved" from death and "raised up" to life and health.

And if he has committed sins (hamartia), he will be forgiven: This would appear to be a conditional effect of the rite. By the forgiveness of sins, serious sins are intended. Once again, a close relationship exists between bodily and spiritual sickness, for in both the Jewish and Christian Bible, physical healing and forgiveness of sins are closely associated. Some commentators, including Fathers of the Church such as Origen, Chrysostom, and Bede, as well as the Council of Trent, see a relationship here to the penitential discipline of the Church.[15]

Therefore confess your sins to one another, and pray for one another, that you may be healed. The prayer of a righteous man has great power in its effects: After mention of forgiveness of sins, there follows a general exhortation to mutual confession. The connection with the preceding section of James is not totally clear. Dibelius considers this an interpolation by the author into an older saying held together by the association of ideas. In view of the relationship in the Jewish mind between sin and bodily infirmity, the restoration could include both the healing from sin as well as from bodily affliction.

In summary, James refers to an action to be performed by ministers of the Church (presbyters) for the benefit of sick Christians. The rite consists of the prayer of faith conjoined with an anointing with oil. Already present are implications for a later understanding of the sacramental sign: the liturgical word of the prayer of faith ("form") and the liturgical action of the anointing ("matter"). The results of this ministration are described in verbs cast in the future tense: "to save," "to raise up," "to heal" (v. 16). The context does not require these to be interpreted in a purely eschatological spiritual sense, that is save from sin, raise up from the dead, a future spiritual healing. On the other hand, neither do they seem to connote a purely bodily, medicinal result. Rather the effects touch the entire religious situation of the sick person: the threat to salvation posed by religious powerlessness and weakness of soul, as well as the temptation to abandon one's trust and faith. The sick person will be raised up from this weakness and saved from this threat of sickness to salvation. The conditional effect of forgiveness of sins is conditional precisely because the recipient of anointing need not be a sinner in the sense understood in verse 15b.

FIRST 800 YEARS: RITE FOR THE SICK
The sources for the anointing of the sick in the first 800 years of Christian history are found in liturgical blessings for oil, patristic writings, and hagiographical accounts. These have been exhaustively researched by A. Chavasse in his landmark study of anointing in the Latin Church.[16]

Liturgical Sources
Chavasse examined thirteen liturgical texts found in Roman, Milanese, Gallican, Visigothic, Irish, and English sources. All of them are associated with the blessing or preparation of the oil. The earliest text relating unmistakably to the anointing of the sick is the blessing of oil found in the *Apostolic Tradition* of Hippolytus of Rome (c. 215):

"V. 1.   If anyone offers oil, he [the Bishop] shall make eucharist [or, *render thanks*] as at the oblation of the bread and wine. But he shall not say word for word [*the same prayer*] but with similiar effect saying:

"2. God who sanctifiest this oil, as Thou dost grant
unto all who are anointed and receive of it the
hallowing wherewith Thou didst anoint kings [*and*]
priests and prophets, so [*grant that*] it may give
strength to all that taste of it and health to all that use
it."[17]

The oil was presented by the faithful, a Roman custom
until the eighth century. The blessing takes place
during the eucharist conducted by the bishop, who
was assisted by his presbyterium. Like most blessings
it is both anamnetic and epicletic; that is, it both recalls
by way of memorial the use of oil in salvation history
(anointing of kings, priests, and prophets) and invokes
the power of God upon the oil. Thus sanctified, the oil
becomes capable of producing its healing effects for
those who use it. Just as the faithful would bring the
eucharist home with them for communion during the
week, so also would they take the blessed oil home
and apply it to themselves either through the form of
drink ("taste") or through external application. The
implied results were strength and health. While there
is the possibility that some of the oil would be used by
ministers of the Church in visiting the sick, this is not
stated explicitly.

The *Apostolic Tradition* has exerted a widespread
influence on both the Western and the Eastern
Churches. Also from an Eastern Church is the Prayer
Book of Serapion (c. 350), who was bishop of Thmuis
in Egypt and a close friend of Athanasius. Serapion's
Euchologion contains three blessings for oil: oil and
water offered by the faithful; chrism with which the
baptized are anointed; and the blessing for oil of the
sick or for bread or for water. The blessing last
mentioned, reproduced below, has a confusing title,
for the prayer deals almost exclusively with the oil, and
not with bread or water.

"We invoke Thee, who hast all power and might, Saviour of all men, Father of our Lord and Saviour Jesus Christ, and we pray Thee to send down from the heavens of Thy Only-begotten a curative power upon this oil, in order that to those who are anointed with these Thy creatures or who receive them, it may become a means of removing 'every disease and every sickness,' of warding off every demon, of putting to flight every unclean spirit, of keeping at a distance every evil spirit, of banishing all fever, all chill, and all weariness; a means of grace and goodness and the remission of sins; a medicament of life and salvation, unto health and soundness of soul and body and spirit, unto perfect well-being."[18]

Perfect well-being are the words that best summarize the purpose of this anointing. Its comprehensiveness aims at a wholeness that includes the removal of every disease and sickness, the exorcistic casting out of demons and unclean spirits, and a means of grace and remission of sins.

Another important prayer of blessing for the Western Church is the *Emitte* Prayer, which is thought to date from the beginning of the fifth century. Found in the Gelasian and Gregorian sacramentaries, it is substantially the same prayer used in the Roman Pontifical for blessing oil until as recently as 1970. In all likelihood, the oil was originally blessed toward the end of the Roman Canon, the same position it occupies in the Chrism Mass today, where reference is made to all "these gifts" (*haec dona*) which are filled with life and goodness, blessed and made holy.

"Send down from heaven, we beseech Thee, Lord, the Holy Spirit, the Paraclete, upon the richness of this oil, which Thou hast designed to bring forth from the green tree for refreshment of mind and body. And may Thy blessing be to all who anoint, taste, and touch a protection for body, soul, and spirit, for dispelling all sufferings, all sickness, all illness of mind and body. With this oil Thou didst anoint priests, kings, and prophets and martyrs; Thy perfect chrism, blessed by Thee, O Lord, and remaining within our inner organs, in the name of our Lord Jesus Christ. Through whom all these good gifts, O Lord, Thou dost ever create."[19]

The invocation of the Holy Spirit (*Emitte*) at the beginning of this prayer indicates its strong epicletic character. Oil is already predisposed as a healing remedy: brought forth "from the green tree for refreshment of mind and body." As a result of the blessing, the natural properties of oil are transformed, given a new efficacy, a new dignity: "Thy perfect chrism," oil with which priests, kings, prophets, and martyrs are anointed. The blessed oil is a healing remedy for the total person: "a protection for body, soul, and spirit," which dispels all suffering, sickness, and illness of mind and body. The manner of application is varied: "anoint, taste, and touch." The active voice suggests that the faithful make the application.

Patristic and Hagiographical Texts
How widespread was the practice of anointing the sick with oil? It is noteworthy that Augustine in his huge corpus of writings nowhere mentioned this custom. The first patristic text to invoke the authority of James in reference to the actual practice of anointing is the celebrated letter of Pope Innocent to Decentius, bishop of Gubbio. This letter, dating from the year 416, is of great importance for the development of anointing, as well as for confirmation, in the Western Church. Through the intermediary of the deacon Celestine, Decentius consulted the bishop of Rome regarding liturgical procedures. The document, as is most of the patristic evidence, is of an occasional nature designed

to answer two specific questions: who is the recipient of anointing, and who is the minister. Answering the first question, Innocent agrees with the proposed interpretation of the letter of James:

"Now there is no doubt that these words are to be understood of the faithful who are sick, and who can be anointed with the holy oil of chrism, which has been prepared by the bishop, and which not only priests, but all Christians may use for anointing, when their own needs or those of their family demand."[20]

In answer to the second question concerning the minister, there is an implied criticism of the proposed interpretation that the presbyters of James might not include the local bishop. To this Innocent continues:

". . . if the bishop either can, or deems it proper that he should, visit someone in person, surely he whose office it is to prepare the chrism can both bless and anoint with chrism. But he cannot pour it on penitents, since it is a kind of sacrament. And how can it be deemed proper to grant one kind of sacrament to those who are denied the rest of the sacraments?"

From this passage it appears that anointing of the sick was an established custom at Rome. The preparation (conficitur) of oil was reserved to the bishop. The application of the blessed oil could be done by lay people, by presbyters, or by the bishop himself. Since the blessed oil was a "kind of sacrament" (genus sacramenti), it is not to be given to penitents and catechumens, but only to the faithful in good standing.

If Innocent reflects the tradition of the Church in Rome concerning anointing, the Church in Gaul is represented by Caesarius of Arles (d. 543) and Elgius of Noyon (d. 659). Caesarius exhorts his people in time of sickness to put their trust in the eucharist and the oil for the sick rather than to rely on the incantations of sorcerers. He makes passing reference to anointing in several of his homilies:

"How much more correct and salutary it would be to hurry to the church, to receive the body and blood of Christ, and with oil that is blessed to anoint in all faith themselves and their dear ones; for according to what James the Apostle says, not only would they receive health of body, but also the remission of sins. For through him the Holy Spirit has made the following promise: 'If anyone is sick. . . .'"[21]

In addition to encouraging lay anointings, presumably at home, Caesarius also refers to anointing in church by priests assisted by deacons:

"As often as one is taken by sickness [he says], let him get to church and receive the Body and Blood of Christ and be anointed by the priests with blessed oil. Let them ask the priests and deacons to pray over them in Christ's Name, which will bring them both health of the body and the remission of sins. For the Lord has been pleased to promise this through His Apostle James, saying: 'If a man falls sick . . . .'"[22]

It is a question throughout of supplanting magical rites of healing among people of a pagan culture still very much in need of evangelization. Instead of resorting to sinful pagan practices of healing, one should hurry to the church to receive the Christian healing rites of the eucharist and oil of anointing, where one will obtain both healing of body and remission of sins. The eucharist is always mentioned in conjunction with anointing. Could it be that the practice of taking those two blessed elements home from the Sunday eucharistic assembly still perdured? The remission of sins is not further specified; it could be understood as a reaction to sinful heathen practices that involve the death of the soul. Of interest is the perennial phenomenon that healing practices can easily become part of a people's religion, at times bordering on magical superstition.

In the seventh century, Eligius, bishop of Noyon in southern France, almost as if repeating the exhortation of Caesarius, urges his faithful to trust in the eucharist and the blessed oil of the Church rather than in magical remedies. Once again, lay anointing is given prominence, that is, self-anointing with oil blessed by the bishop:

"As often as any sickness shall occur, let them not seek out the sorcerers . . . but let the sick person put his trust in the mercy of God alone, so as to receive with faith and devotion the Eucharist of the body and blood of Christ, and with confidence to ask the Church for blessed oil, with which he may anoint his body in the name of the Lord; and, according to the Apostle, 'the prayer of faith will save the sick man, and the Lord will raise him up'; and he will receive not only health of body but also of soul; and there will be realized in him what the Lord has promised in the Gospel, saying 'And all things whatever you ask for in prayer, believing, you shall receive.'"[23]

From the Church in England in the eighth century comes the witness of Venerable Bede (+735). In his commentary on the epistle of James, the first of its kind, Bede repeats the now traditional character of the rite referring to the authority of Innocent of Rome and reflecting the Roman tradition:

"Is anyone among you sick?, etc. Just as he had given advice to one who was sad, so to one who is sick . . . to the effect that one who suffers greater temptation should be mindful to cure himself with the help of many, and particularly with the help of older men [seniorum] . . .

"And let them pray over him, anointing him, etc. In the Gospel we read that the Apostles also did this, and even now the custom of the Church holds that the sick are to be anointed by presbyters with consecrated oil, and to be healed by the accompanying prayer. Not only presbyters, but as Pope Innocent writes, all Christians as well may use this same oil for anointing, when their own needs or those of family demand. However, this oil may be prepared [*confici*] only by bishops. For the saying, 'with oil in the name of the Lord,' means oil consecrated in the name of the Lord. At least it means that when they anoint the sick man, they ought to invoke over him the name of the Lord."[24]

The composition of the rite, its effects, the persons qualified to anoint, and the preparation of oil remain as before. What is new is the chronological—and originally etymological—interpretation of "presbyter" as elder or older men (*seniorum*). Bede also interprets James 5:15b and 16 with reference to confession of sins: more serious sins are to be confessed to the presbyters; lighter offenses and daily sins may be confessed to one another.

In addition to these patristic citations, accounts of anointing with oil can be found in the lives of saints. For example, Suplicius Severus tells of the wife of a nobleman named Avitus who asked St. Martin of Tours to bless "as is the custom" a vessel of oil intended as a remedy for sickness.[25] Similarly, St. Genevieve was accustomed to anointing with blessed oil the sick for whom she cared. One day when she needed the oil and found the vessel empty, she was panic stricken "because there was no bishop within reach to bless the oil."[26] It could be that the rite of simple blessing of oil from the *Rituale Romanum* of 1614 is a vestige of this earlier practice.

Conclusions

Chavasse makes some telling conclusions regarding the anointing of the sick in the first 800 years in the Western Church.[27]

The Relationship between the Blessing and the Application of the Oil

It was necessary that the oil used to anoint the sick be blessed: "blessed oil," "holy oil," "sacred oil," "prepared oil." A primordial importance was attached to the blessing of the oil, which placed it in the category of a "sacrament" (Innocent), although the reader must be careful not to read into this term a more technical definition of the seven sacraments as evolved in the twelfth and thirteenth centuries. The efficacy of the oil is related to its blessing. Somewhat analogous to the waters of baptism and the oil of chrism, the prayer of epiclesis imbued the oil with a divine power. In other words, the oil is efficacious as a result of the blessing; the anointing with the blessed oil simply offered an occasion to apply its intrinsic power. Recall that the Fathers all deemed the consecration of the oil by the bishop a more important issue than who applied it. Furthermore, the earliest liturgical sources have to do with the preparation or blessing of the oil; rituals of its application cannot be dated earlier than the eighth century. While the preparation and blessing of the oil was strictly reserved to the bishop, the application of the oil was not restricted only to ordained ministers. The liturgical forms of blessing seem to presume a self-application of oil. Although Innocent and Bede distinguish two types of unction, lay and presbyteral, no great difference is made between the two. Oftentimes when oil was to be applied by another, the tendency was to seek out someone who had a reputation for holiness or who possessed a charism of healing.[28]

The Practice of Blessing and Applying the Oil

The use of fixed formulas for blessing the oil is very ancient in the Latin Church, but not, however, for its application. Only the blessing of oil is liturgically organized before the middle of the eighth century. As far as one can determine, the oil was applied in varying ways. External usage (*ungere, tangere*) was most frequent, usually by application to the ailing member of the body. Internal usage was also practiced: the *Emitte* speaks of drinking the oil, which remains "in our inward parts" (*in visceribus nostris*). Sometimes the imposition of hands accompanied the anointing; more often before the ninth century, the laying on of hands was performed independently of the anointing. As for the prayer that accompanied the anointing, sometimes there were prayers before the actual anointing; the prayer coinciding with the anointing itself often invoked Christ or the Trinity.

Results of Unction

Anointing is given only to the baptized, and among them, according to Innocent, only to those who are not liable to the public penitential discipline. A later sacramental theology would say that anointing was a sacrament for the living. The corporeal or bodily effects of anointing receive particular emphasis. Of the thirteen prayers of blessing analyzed by Chavasse, the five oldest mention no spiritual effect; three pray for the effect on the spirit; the five most recent introduce a petition for pardon of sins. Anointing of the sick does not appear to be a preparatory rite for death; before the ninth century there is no mention of unction in *extremis*; after that transitional period it occurs very frequently. While the earliest documents stress the bodily effects of anointing, there is already in antiquity a development in the understanding that anointing has some relationship to the forgiveness of sins, however understood.

Commenting on these findings, A. Knauber thinks that the expected results are not simply bodily healing but a deeper wholeness: strength, forgiveness of sins, vivification, protection of body, mind, and spirit. In other words, what is involved is the entire somatic realm of salvation for a sick person battling with demonic powers while reaching out to the indwelling of the Holy Spirit and the power of Christ.[29]

Reference to James
The practice of anointing, according to Chavasse, is seen in direct relation to the prescription of James 5:14–16 by virtually all the Church Fathers and by some of the prayers of blessing. In all honesty, however, we have at least two unanswered questions. One has to do with the interpretation of "presbyters" in James 5, originally taken to mean officeholders in the primitive Jerusalem Church. The allusion to James by way of validation for the practice of anointing the sick in the first 800 years of the Western Church is not entirely consistent, since the application of the oil prepared by the bishop was not restricted to presbyters but was available to all the baptized. The other question concerns the importance attached to the episcopal preparation or blessing of the oil for imbuing it with a divine efficacy, a shift in emphasis far removed from the anointing with oil and the expectant prayer of faith enjoined by James. More specifically, the implied sacramental theology is a more static one concerned with holy or blessed things rather than the dynamic symbolic action of applying the oil "in the name of the Lord" as James urged. Moreover, for James the accompanying prayer of faith is accorded more importance than the actual anointing: it is the "prayer of faith" that "saves" the sick person.

CAROLINGIAN TURNING POINT
The oldest extant full ritual for the actual anointing of

the sick has been identified by H. B. Porter as a Carolingian compilation from Roman, Gallican, and Mozarabic or Spanish sources between the years 815 and 845.[30] The celebration appears to be a communal participated liturgy that included sung chants.

The liturgy begins as the priests prepare the salt and water to be blessed and sprinkled over the sick person and the home. This introductory rite of sprinkling with holy water, taken from Benedict of Aniane's Supplement to the Sacramentary of Hadrian, was exorcistic and intended to rid the environment of any influence of demonic powers thought to be at work in human illness. Six short collects follow, likewise from the Supplement, and a longer prayer of Carolingian provenance, *Domine Deus qui per apostolum*, which begins with a reference to James' prescription to call for the presbyters:

"Lord God, who hast spoken by Thine Apostle James, saying: Is any one sick among you? Let him call in the presbyters of the Church, and let them pray over him, anointing him with oil in the name of the Lord; and the prayer of faith shall save the sick man, and the Lord will raise him up; and if he be in sins, they shall be forgiven him: cure, we beseech Thee, our Redeemer, by the grace of the Holy Spirit, the weakness of this sick man; heal his wounds, and forgive his sins; drive out from him all pains of body and mind, and mercifully restore to him full health, both inwardly and outwardly; that recovered and healed by the help of Thy mercy, he may be strengthened to take up again his former duties of piety to Thee."[31]

The ailing Christian is then instructed to genuflect and stand at the priest's right where hands are laid upon him, while antiphons, psalms (50, 120, 38), and prayers taken largely from Mozarabic sources are said or sung. The rubric for the actual anointing is interesting for its incarnational flexibility:

"And let him anoint the sick man with sanctified oil, making signs of the cross on the [back of the] neck and on the throat, and between the shoulders and on the breast; or let him anoint further the place where the pain is more pronounced. . . ."

A Gallican prayer of anointing follows:

"I anoint thee with holy oil in the name of the Father and of the Son and of the Holy Spirit, that the unclean spirit may not remain hidden in thee, nor in thy members; rather, through the working of this mystery, may there dwell in thee the power of Christ, all-high, and of the Holy Spirit. And through this ointment of consecrated oil and our prayer, cured and warmed by the Holy Spirit mayest thou merit to receive thy former and even better health."

After a long prayer and short petition that God be propitious, both Mozarabic, the rubrics direct:

"Then let him communicate him with the body and blood of the Lord. And let them do the same for seven days, if there be need, both with regard to communion as well as the other office; and the Lord will raise him up, and, if he be in sins, they will be forgiven him."

This "other office" is generally understood to be the anointing, which would thus be repeatable. A further rubric, related to the Mozarabic usage, suggests that the office for the sick with its hours in the morning and evening, together with the hymn "Christ, medicine of the heavenly Father" (*Christe coelestis medicina Patris*), be prayed on each of the days as well.

Appended to this liturgy of anointing in many subsequent manuscripts is a further rubric, which is symptomatic of a change beginning to work in Carolingian circles that would alter profoundly the later history of anointing:

"Now many priests anoint the sick also on the five senses, that is, on the eyelids, and on the inner nostrils and on the tip of the nose or externally, and on the outside of the lips and on the outside or the back of the hands. Accordingly, on all these members let them make the sign of the cross with sacred oil, saying; In the name of the Father and of the Son, and of the Holy Spirit."

In the kingdom of the Franks under Charlemagne a reform movement was under way at Aachen which, among its other goals, involved the renewal of priestly ministry and the abandonment of the practice of lay anointings.

Canon 48 of the Council of Chalon II (813) describes this development:

"According to the document of the Apostle James, with which the documents of the Fathers are also in agreement, the sick ought to be anointed by presbyters with oil which is blessed by the bishop. For thus he says: *Is anyone among you sick.* . . . Accordingly, a remedy of this kind, which heals the weaknesses of soul and body, is not to be lightly regarded."[32]

Other local synods held at Aachen (836) and Mainz (847) also lent strong support to the practice of presbyteral anointing. Chapter 8 of the Council of Pavia (850) associates this growing custom more closely with other rites for the dying: namely, deathbed reconciliation and viaticum.

"That salutary sacrament, which James the Apostle commends, saying: 'Is anyone among you sick,' is also to be made known to the people by assiduous preaching: surely it is a great mystery and greatly to be desired; through it, if one asks with confidence, [sins] are remitted and, as a result, bodily health restored. But since it often happens that some sick person either

24

may not know the force of the sacrament or, believing his sickness to be less dangerous than it is, pretends to co-operate in his salvation, or may be unaware of the virulence of the disease, the local presbyter ought to admonish him in a fitting manner . . . but it must be understood that if the sick person is bound by public penance, he cannot receive the remedy of this mystery, unless he has first received reconciliation and is worthy of the communion of the body and blood of Christ. For he to whom the other sacraments are forbidden is in no way allowed to use this one."[33]

This is what appears to have happened. By the year 800, the practice of deathbed penance, the final disintegration of the public penitential discipline of the early Church before the advent of the Celtic private penance, was widespread and was, of course, administered only by presbyters or bishops. At the same time, the practice of anointing the sick by presbyters was only then becoming liturgically organized. With the Carolingian emphasis on the priestly ministry, the anointing of the sick by lay people gradually disappeared. The new rite of anointing began to be performed at the same time as the already established rites of deathbed penance, for Pope Innocent had decreed many years earlier that anointing was to be withheld from public penitents, who first had to be reconciled. Thus the key factors in the transition from the first 800 years to the Middle Ages are the rise of an organized ritual of anointing increasingly entrusted to presbyters, and the association of this anointing ritual with deathbed reconciliation of penitents. As a result, anointing in the Middle Ages is characterized by a spiritualizing tendency reflected in the growing emphasis on remission of sins, wherein the effects of deathbed penance and anointing are confused. Anointing of the sick thus becomes a sacrament for the dying by association with *paenitentia ad mortem*. Anointing became even more "extreme unction" after the twelfth century, when the original order of sacraments was changed from penance, anointing, viaticum, to penance, viaticum, anointing.

To look at this development in more detail, the systematic organization of the ritual of anointing began at the end of the eighth century, with texts drawn from the Gelasian and Gregorian sacramentaries, such as had gone into the Supplement to the papal Sacramentary of Hadrian, while absorbing other material from Gelasian rites of penance.[34] The first and logical matrix for this organized ritual were prayers for visiting the sick. The inclusion of penance had to take into account the two stages of admission to penance and the subsequent reconciliation, when possible, which were two distinct ceremonies separated in time. Taking its place among the rites of *paenitentia ad mortem*, anointing always followed the admission to penance; sometimes it followed and sometimes it preceded actual reconciliation. When deathbed reconciliation lost its original purpose and was replaced by a simple private penance, unction annexed to itself the prayers and particular discipline earlier attached to penance. As far as association of anointing with viaticum, the development went in one of two directions: either the anointing was incorporated into a "Mass" of communion for the sick (really a *missa sicca* without a canon or consecration) or, which was more often the case, viaticum became a part of the ritual of anointing.

The once simple form of anointing was thus expanded into an elaborate service, especially in monasteries, with this progression of components: the blessing and sprinkling of holy water, many psalms (often the seven penitential psalms) and prayers, penance, anointing, viaticum, and the blessing and clothing with a penitential hairshirt by way of penitential expiation. In the tenth century, a reaction set in against this unwieldy ritual, emanating from the Benedictine monks at Cluny. This led to a further simplification found in the Pontifical of the Roman Curia of the thirteenth century, which was propagated throughout Western Europe by the Franciscan friars. In this abridged order (*ordo compendiosus*), the prayers pertaining to deathbed penance were removed, with only the penitential psalms and litanies remaining. The many prayers connected with anointing were likewise eliminated, and a distinction was made between visiting the sick, anointing, and viaticum. This simplified rite was further modified in the *Liber Sacerdotalis* of Alberto Castellani (d. c. 1522) and the ritual of Cardinal Santorius (d. 1602), which were the immediate forerunners of the *Rituale Romanum* of 1614. The order for extreme unction in the Ritual used until the reform of the Second Vatican Council consisted of the opening sprinkling; penance, when necessary; three prayers at the entrance to the house; the anointing; and three prayers taken from visiting the sick.

As for the anointing itself in the medieval rite, Chavasse has isolated three types of rituals. The rituals of Type I correspond substantially to the Carolingian order reproduced above. The rituals of Type II are a further evolution from Type I and can be dated from the middle of the ninth century. A mark distinguishing them from Type I is that each anointing has a proper prayer. They are, in turn, similar to the rituals of Type III, except for two features: the anointings are not yet limited to the five senses and the accompanying prayer is indicative: for example, "I anoint your eyes with blessed oil, so that however you have sinned by improper sight, may be expiated by the anointing of this oil." The rituals of Type III, originating at the end of the tenth century, constitute the simplification found in the Roman Pontifical of the thirteenth century and the practice in use until 1972. They provide for anointings of the five senses with a deprecative form: for example, "May the Lord forgive you by this holy + anointing and His most loving mercy whatever sins you have committed by the use of your sight (etc.) Amen."

One final question: how much did the people avail themselves of the sacrament of anointing during the Middle Ages? How widespread was its frequency among the faithful? At certain times it appears that anointing fell into desuetude. Not only did its protracted length discourage potential recipients, but also the cupidity and greed of many priests who demanded extravagant stole fees and who even kept the linen sheets and candles used during the anointing. It is a sad commentary on pastoral care that in some circles it was said that only a person who owned two cows could afford to ask for the sacrament.[35]

THE SCHOLASTICS: SACRAMENT OF THE DYING
The early scholastic period was divided in its teaching on anointing. One tradition still maintained that the alleviation of physical illness was one of the purposes of the sacrament. Citing the text of James, Hugh of St. Victor (d. 1141) held that the sacrament was instituted for a twofold reason, the remission of sins and the alleviation of bodily sickness:

"Hence it is clear that he who receives this anointing faithfully and with devotion unquestionably merits to receive through it alleviation and consolation both in body and soul, provided, however, that it is expedient that he be alleviated in both."[36]

Roland Bandinelli (d. 1181), the future Pope Alexander III, claimed that the sacrament "was instituted for this reason, that through it certain sins might be remitted and the sick man might convalesce more quickly and be restored to health."[37] Omnebene (d. 1185), his contemporary, taught that the reality or grace of the sacrament is "the remission of sins and, at times, the health of the body and the bestowal of other goods."[38] William of Auxere (d. 1231) summed up his reflections by stating that "the principal and proper effect of this sacrament is the cure of the body . . . but the most excellent effect is the remission of sins."[39]

The other tradition among the early schoolmen held that anointing was a sacrament of the dying, to be administered at the time of departure from this life. The reality or grace was restricted to the remission of sins. The *Epitome theologiae christianae,* attributed to Master Herman, a disciple of Peter Abelard, described the sacrament as "the last of all and, so to speak, the final consummation." The medieval extreme unction is already taking shape as he continues:

"Every Christian is anointed three times: first, for his inception, namely in baptism; secondly, in confirmation, where the gifts of grace are conferred; thirdly, on departing [*in exitu*], where if sins are present, they are remitted in whole or in major part."[40]

The anonymous author of the *Summa sententiarum,* like Omnebene, developed the effect of unction in terms of the reality or grace symbolized by the outward anointing; unlike Omnebene, he restricted the grace of anointing to the remission of sins.[41] Master Simon was the first to state that this sacrament of the departing prepares the soul for the beatific vision. Drawing a parallel between baptism and unction, he wrote: "Baptism seals those who enter this world with the character of Christ; unction presents those who are departing this world for the divine vision."[42] Peter Lombard (d. 1160) was the first to use the term "extreme unction" for what Hugh of St. Victor had called the sacrament of the anointing of the sick.

The scholastics were commenting on the practice and liturgy of unction as they experienced it in their day; already in the ninth century, it had undergone a change from a rite for the sick to a rite for the dying. The patristic and liturgical documents of the first 800 years were largely neglected or unavailable; they are seldom, if ever, cited. In their systematic development of sacramental theology, a number of crucial questions arose touching on Christian anthropology. How can a physical effect, the recovery of health, be an effect of a sacrament? Sacraments are means of grace, and grace is a supernatural perfection. Furthermore, if sacraments always produce their effect in a disposed subject, how can the recovery of health, a result seldom realized, be the effect of this sacrament? All these difficulties were resolved by concluding that the remission of sins was the principal effect of unction. Yet two sacraments already had this purpose of forgiving sins: baptism with reference to original sin, and penance for personal sin. Thus the logical conclusion was to regard unction as destined for the removal of sin's last remnants, to delay its reception to the final moments of life, and to consider it as extreme unction. William of Auvergne summed up the purpose of anointing as it came to be accepted by all the scholastic doctors of the thirteenth and fourteenth centuries:

"Now since those who are departing this world are soon to be presented to God, it is not proper to doubt that they are to be sanctified from those faults which have clung to them while in this world, just as dust clings to the feet of the wayfarer, and from those slight and daily blemishes which are usually called venial sins; for a bride never approaches the bridegroom without some preparatory ablutions and fitting attire.

30

. . . And since those who are about to die are like the bride who is about to enter the chamber of the bridegroom . . . it is clear to men of understanding how necessary and how fitting is the sacrament of the last hallowing [extremae sanctificationis]. Again, since those who have been sanctified are, as it were, recruited for a holy and spiritual war, and since there still remains the most bitter of struggles and wars against the demon . . . who shall doubt how necessary is strength and renewed vitality: strength, I mean, by which they may manfully win a resounding victory against their enemies and forcefully put them to flight."[43]

The point of departure for determining the grace or principal effect of the sacrament is henceforth unction as a preparation for glory.

A controversy did take place between the Dominican school of Albert the Great and Thomas Aquinas, and the Franciscan school of Bonaventure and Scotus. Both schools agreed that the principal effect of the sacrament was the remission of sins. The Franciscans held, however, that unction had to do with the forgiveness of venial sins; the Dominicans claimed that it was for the remission of the remnants (reliquiae) of sin which impeded the soul's passage to glory. In the words of Aquinas, the principal effect of unction was the spiritual cure of those "failings which render a man spiritually sick, with the result that he has not that perfect strength needed for leading a life of grace and glory. Now this failing is nothing else but a debility and inability of sorts, which is left as the result of actual or original sin."[44]

They are all of one mind, however, that this sacrament for the dying prepares the soul for heaven. Both Albert and Thomas held that the recipient of anointing must be in "a state of departure." For Albert, the extreme

(last) unction has become the last (extreme) sacrament;
for Thomas, anointing is the Church's last remedy.
Bonaventure and Scotus went so far as to demand the
very imminence of death as necessary for the reception
of unction. Bonaventure insisted it be given only
"where danger of death is imminent" and only to
those "who are as it were in transit to another state."[45]
Duns Scotus (d. 1308) completed this development of
anointing from a rite for the sick to a sacrament of the
dying when he stated that it "is to be given only to
such as a sick person who is no longer capable of
sinning and who is in danger of death."[46] In other
words, the proper time for the sacrament is *in extremis*,
in the agony of death, because the recipient is unable
to sin further and thus cannot negate the effect of the
sacrament.

The Reunion Council of Florence, in its Decree for the
Armenians (1439), provides a good summary of the
scholastic teaching on extreme unction of the later
Middle Ages. Although largely Thomistic in its
orientation, the Decree does not completely ignore the
reflections of the earliest schoolmen, perhaps as a
concession to the practice and theology of the Eastern
Church.

"The fifth sacrament is extreme unction. Its matter is
olive oil blessed by the bishop. This sacrament may not
be given except to a sick person whose life is feared
for. He is to be anointed on these parts: on the eyes on
account of sight, on the ears on account of hearing, on
the nostrils on account of smelling, on the mouth on
account of taste and speech, on the hands on account
of touch, on the feet on account of movement, on the
loins on account of the lust seated there.

"The minister of this sacrament is the priest. The effect
is the healing of the mind, and as far as it is good for
the soul, of the body as well. Of this sacrament blessed
James the apostle says: 'Is any among you sick . . .'"[47]

Martin Luther, in his *Babylonian Captivity,* claimed that
unction was not a sacrament instituted by Christ, but
could be a means of stimulating faith in forgiveness.[48]
There is preserved, however, a remarkable letter
written in the last year of his life to a pastor giving
advice on how to minister to the sick. Luther suggests
a home visitation with two or three good men
involving common prayer and the laying on of hands,
which is to take place three times a day together with
public prayers in the church.[49] John Calvin taught that
anointing pertained to a miraculous gift of healing that
accompanied the first preaching of the gospel, a gift
not communicated to subsequent generations. Even if
the precept of unction did pertain to the present age,
for Calvin, the Roman practice with the superstitious
blessing of oil and anointing of "half-dead carcasses"
was an abuse of the anointing encouraged by James.[50]

The Council of Trent addressed itself to issues such as
these at the fourteenth session in 1551, a teaching that
followed immediately upon a consideration of
penance. The Council Fathers devoted three chapters
to extreme unction: the institution of extreme unction,
the effect of the sacrament, and the minister and time
of administration.[51] Of greater dogmatic significance
are the four canons.[52] First of all, extreme unction is a
sacrament instituted by Christ and announced by
James. Second, it has an enduring salvific meaning in
terms of conferring grace, remitting sins, and
comforting the sick. Third, the rite and practice of the
sacrament correspond with the scriptural precedent in
James. Fourth, the proper minister of anointing is an
ordained priest.

Especially noteworthy is that, although indebted to
scholastic terminology, Trent stopped short of
canonizing the one-sided approach of the later
schoolmen regarding unction as a sacrament of the

dying. The original draft of November 16, 1551, read that extreme unction is to be administered "only [*dumtaxat*] to those who are in their final struggle and have come to grips with death and are about to go forth to the Lord." The definitive text was providentially changed: "this anointing is to be administered to the sick, especially [*praesertim*] to those who are so dangerously ill that they seem near to death."[53] Furthermore, the canons of Trent say nothing specific about the rite's function as a sacrament of the dying or about the degree of sickness. Three times the word sick (*infirmi*), not dying (*moribundi*), is used. Finally, Trent taught that the graced effect of unction is not merely remission of sins. No mention is even made of a primary effect. The stress is rather on the grace of the Holy Spirit with a possible threefold result: (1) the sacrament takes away sin and its remains; (2) it raises up the soul of the sick person by exciting confidence in divine mercy, so that he or she may bear more lightly the miseries of illness and resist more easily the temptation of the devil; and (3) when expedient for the welfare of the body, it may even restore bodily health. These spiritual, psychological, and physical benefits look to the strengthening of the entire human person in time of sickness.

In the *Rituale Romanum* of 1614, Title VI was devoted to the sacrament of extreme unction. Its contents actually included much more: introductory notes on the sacrament, the rite of its ministration, the seven penitential psalms with the litany of the saints, pastoral suggestions on visiting and caring for the sick, the manner of assisting the dying, the order of commendation of a soul, and the final *De exspiratione* at the moment of death. Upon closer examination, the various components came from three sources: (1) liturgical rites, (2) devotional forms, in particular the tender piety of the fifteenth century for the passion of

Christ, and (3) pastoral suggestions reflecting the special concerns of the Counter-Reformation in Italy. The communion of the sick, which more and more was associated with viaticum, is found under an altogether different section, Title V on the sacrament of the eucharist. Additional blessings for the sick and dying are found under Title IX in this logically laid out, but pastorally awkward, arrangement of euchological material. And lest we forget, not the least of pastoral difficulties was the Latin language, generally unknown to the people!

The post-Tridentine era was marked by a progressive leniency concerning the interpretation of the danger of death required for anointing, and by the consequent restoration of extreme unction as a sacrament for sick people. The Catechism of the Council of Trent taught that it was "a very serious sin to defer Holy Unction until, all hope of recovering being lost, life begins to ebb, and the sick person is fast verging into a state of insensibility."[54] The Catechism also censures an implicit lack of faith in the healing power of the sacrament, stating that the "recovery of health, if indeed advantageous, is another effect of the sacrament."[55]

Popes of this century appealed repeatedly for anointing sooner rather than later. Benedict XV, in an Apostolic Letter *Sodalitatem* (May 31, 1921), instructed sodalists that in keeping with the Church's teaching and precepts, the sick are to be strengthened by the sacraments "as soon as the sickness becomes more serious and one can prudently judge that there is danger of death."[56] Pius XI, in his Apostolic Letter *Explorata Res* (February 2, 1923), clarified "prudently" to be understood as "probably":

"For it is not necessary either for the validity or the liceity of the sacrament that death be feared as something proximate; rather it is enough that there be a prudent or probable judgment of danger. And if in such conditions unction ought to be given, in the same conditions it surely can be given."[57]

Without wishing to play with words, the usual condition for the administration of unction continued to be the prudent or probable judgment regarding the very imminence of death itself, not a judgment about the *danger* of death posed by serious illness, as the popes had taught. Priests continued to be called out too late to be of genuine assistance to the sick, who were by then already unconscious or even dead. A morbidity and fatalism became attached to "extreme unction" and the "last rites" which even the best of pastoral practice was unable to surmount. In all truth, extreme unction became a pastoral failure, quite similar to the waning period of the early Church's public penitential discipline, which became so arduous that the faithful postponed it until their deathbed.

Thus the stage was set for the historic utterances of the Fathers of Vatican II. In addition to preferring the name "anointing of the sick" to "extreme unction" and encouraging that the time of ministration be the beginning of the danger of death from sickness or old age, the Council, in its *Constitution on the Sacred Liturgy*, made two further statements. First, paragraph 74 restored the original sequence of reconciliation, anointing, and viaticum:

"In addition to the separate rites for Anointing of the Sick and for Viaticum, a continuous rite shall be prepared in which a sick man is anointed after he had made his confession and before he receives Viaticum."[58]

The position of viaticum, and not unction, as a sacrament for the dying was thereby thrust into greater prominence. Second, paragraph 75 contained recommendations for adapting the anointings and prayers of the rite itself:

"The number of the anointings is to be adapted to the occasion, and the prayers which belong to the rite of Anointing are to be revised so as to correspond to the varying conditions of the sick who receive the sacrament."[59]

ECUMENICAL EPILOGUE

In addition to the scriptural, traditional, and pastoral reasons for the recovery of anointing as a sacrament for the sick, there may be included a fourth one, ecumenical convergence. Both the Eastern Orthodox and the member churches of the Anglican Communion provide services for anointing the sick.

Almost all the Eastern Churches anoint the sick with oil, the exceptions being the Armenians and Nestorians, where the rite has fallen into disuse, and the Ethiopians, where it is seldom conferred. The rituals for administration are for the most part based on the Eastern Orthodox *Euchologion* and, when fully implemented, are very elaborate.[60] It is a "sobornal" or communal sacrament: as many faithful as possible participate, together with seven priests, seven readings from epistles and gospels, seven prayers, and seven anointings of the sick person in the form of a cross on the brow, the nostrils, the cheeks, the lips, the breast, and on both sides of the hands. The accompanying prayer is addressed to the Father as "Physician of souls and bodies," who sent his Son to heal every infirmity and to deliver us from death. The petition for healing of body and soul is made through the intercession of Mary, the angels, the cross, and the saints, especially those closely associated with healing. This sacrament or mystery—which is variously called "prayer oil" (*euchelaion*), "holy oil," "holy unction," and "rite of the lamp"—has for its principal purpose the spiritual,

37

physical, and mental healing of the sick person whatever the nature or gravity of the illness. It is certainly not the last rites, for the ritual in no way indicates extreme cases. In such instances, the Office at the Parting of the Soul from the Body would be employed. A further extension of anointing the sick is a penitential anointing that takes place on Holy Thursday and is open to all the faithful.

Within the Anglican Communion in this century, a remarkable development has occurred in the restoration to its official service books of a rite for anointing the sick.[61] The first *Book of Common Prayer* of 1549 retained an order of anointing the sick in its office of visitation of the sick. Although the rite of anointing was deleted in the 1552 Prayer Book and subsequent revisions, reform movements of a high church persuasion—the Non-Jurors in the eighteenth century and the Oxford tractarians in the nineteenth century— advocated the revival of anointing as a rite for the sick. Today, under the auspices of a healing ministry, the anointing of the sick and the laying on of hands is practiced in most of the member churches of the Anglican Communion.

The *Book of Common Prayer* for the Episcopal Church in America (1979) contains a Ministration to the Sick consisting of three parts. One or more parts may be used. Part I is a Ministry of the Word thematically arranged with provision for confession or reconciliation. Part II, Laying on of Hands and Anointing, allows the priest to bless the oil. The laying on of hands is accompanied by a choice of two prayers. The anointing is done in this manner:

"If the person is to be anointed, the Priest dips a thumb in the holy oil, and makes the sign of the cross on the sick person's forehead, saying

"N., I anoint you with oil in the Name of the Father, and of the Son, and of the Holy Spirit, Amen."[62]

To this may also be added an abbreviated version of the original 1549 prayer of anointing. In case of necessity, a deacon or lay person may anoint, using oil blessed by a bishop or priest. When the laying on of hands or anointing takes place within a eucharist, it is administered before the sign of peace preliminary to the communion service. Part III, Holy Communion, begins with the offertory. Provision is also made for communion from the reserved sacrament, and if necessary, communion under one kind only. There is even provision for a kind of spiritual communion for a sick Christian unable to ingest either solid food or liquids. Also included in the Ministration to the Sick are prayers for the sick adapted to various occasions—recovery from illness, sick child, before an operation, doctors and nurses, and so on—as well as prayers for use by the sick themselves. A more recent publication, *The Book of Occasional Services*, has further enriched the Episcopal Church with a very hopeful and consoling public service of healing.[63]

The most recent ecumenical development has occurred within the Lutheran synods in North America: namely, the inclusion of the laying on of hands and the anointing of the sick in the *Occasional Services*, a companion to the *Lutheran Book of Worship* (1982). Two services are provided, a "Service of the Word for Healing," cast in a corporate setting, and a simplified order for the home or hospital. Toward the close of the Service of the Word for Healing, after the laying on of hands performed either in silence or accompanied by a prayer, the minister may dip a thumb in the oil, make the sign of the cross on the forehead, and say:

"O God, the giver of health and salvation: As the apostles of our Lord Jesus Christ, at his command,

anointed many that were sick and healed them, send
now your Holy Spirit, that _____ name _____, anointed
with this oil, may in repentance and faith be made
whole; through the same Jesus Christ our Lord.
(Amen.)"[64]

The prayer of anointing for the more private setting
has been simplified:

" _____ Name _____, I anoint you with oil in the name of
the Father, and of the Son, and of the Holy Spirit.
(Amen.)"[65]

A rubric notes that, "The oil used for anointing is olive
oil, to which an aromatic ingredient such as synthetic
oil of cinnamon or oil of bergamot may be added." A
prayer may also be said when the oil has been
prepared.

CONCLUSION
One reason why so few theologians have attempted to
write on the anointing of the sick is the uneven and
complicated tradition of the sacrament. Here is a
summary of the principal developments we have
traced, as far as the best of recent scholarship allows
us.

1. Two passages in the New Testament speak of
anointing the sick: Mark 6:13, which treats of the
apostolic ministry of healing, and James 5:14–15, the
presbyteral rite of anointing, thought to be the origins
of the sacrament. A balanced exegesis of James
indicated that, on the one hand, the context is one of a
sick, not a dying, Christian. On the other hand, the
anointing made "in the name of the Lord," the "prayer
of faith," and the ministry of the presbyters all indicate
that it is not solely a medicinal remedy.
2. The tradition of the first 800 years of anointing
may be garnered from liturgical sources, patristic
writings, and passages from the lives of saints.

Primordial importance was attached to the blessing of the oil by the bishop; indeed, before the ninth century, the prayers of episcopal preparation are the only extant liturgical texts. The application was most likely done in a more informal manner, by either presbyters or by any baptized Christian. The oil could be applied externally or taken internally. The expected results were a wholeness of body, mind, and spirit. In no way was anointing regarded as a rite for the dying.

3. The Carolingian turning point, a shift beginning in the ninth century, was to transform anointing from a rite for the sick into a sacrament for the dying. The context for this development was a Carolingian reform that led to a change in pastoral practice and liturgy. First, a renewal of priestly ministry brought about the abandonment of lay anointing in favor of anointing restricted exclusively to presbyters. Second, a ritual was developed for the presbyteral application of the blessed oil. Third, this newly created rite of anointing was inserted after deathbed reconciliation in such a way that it became ultimately the extreme unction, the last anointing during one's earthly pilgrimage.

4. This change in pastoral practice led to a further change in the theology of anointing. The schoolmen, reflecting on the practice of unction in their day, which was for the most part administered to the dying, recognized that, like all seven sacraments, unction bestows a spiritual grace always conferred *ex opere operato* (infallibly). Although some of the early scholastics still maintained the possibility of the recovery of health, the common teaching of the thirteenth century held that the spiritual effect of unction was the remission of sins: either venial sins (Franciscan school) or the remains of sin (Dominican school).

5. The Council of Trent refused to sanction this medieval theology of anointing as a sacrament for the dying. Instead, the Council Fathers taught that unction

conveyed the grace of the Holy Spirit with its multiple spiritual, psychological, and physical benefits. The door was left open for the reforms of the Second Vatican Council, which recovered the original tradition of anointing as intended for the seriously ill.

NOTES

1. *Acta et Documenta Concilio Oecumenico Vaticano II apparando,* ser. I. *Antepraeparatoria* vol. II, pars II (Vatican City: Typis Polyglottis Vaticanis, 1961) 95–101. For an assessment of this data see Franz Nikolasch, "Das Sakrament der Krankensalbung," *Theologisch-Praktische Quartalschrift* 125 (1977) 144–57.

2. As cited in P.M. Gy, "Le nouveau rituel romain des malades," *La Maison-Dieu* 113 (1973) 33, n. 9 and 10.

"Sacramentum quod communiter 'Extrema Unctio,' nuncupatur, deinceps 'unctio infirmorum' vocabitur; nam non est per se Sacramentum morientium, sed graviter aegrotantium, ac proinde tempus opportunum illud recipendi est statim ac fidelis in gravem morbum inciderit.

"Unctio sacra in diuturna infirmitate aliquando iterari potest."

3. *Constitution on the Sacred Liturgy,* para. 73 (Flannery, p. 22).

4. Josephus Kern, *De sacramento extremae unctionis tractatus dogmaticus* (Regensburg: 1907).

5. F. Tecklenburg, "The Primary Effect of Extreme Unction," *Ecclesiastical Review* 55 (1916) 291–99.

6. H.A. Reinhold, "The Sacrament of Extreme Unction in Parish Life," *The American Parish and the Roman Liturgy,* proceedings of National Liturgical Week 1941, 135–41.

7. Bernhard Poschmann, *Penance and Anointing of the Sick* (New York: Herder, 1964) 233–57. Michael Schmaus, *Katholische Dogmatik* IV/I (Munich, 6th rev. ed. 1964) 695–725. A. Grillmeier, "Das Sakrament der Auferstehung. Versuch einer Sinndeutung der letzten Ölung," *Geist und Leben* 34 (1961) 326–36.

8. Bernard Botte, "L'onction des malades," *La Maison-Dieu* 15 (1948) 91–107. The entire issue was devoted to updating the sacramental ministry to the sick, as was the more recent *La Maison-Dieu* 113 (1973), "Le nouveau rituel des malades."

9. Bo Reicke, "L'onction des malades d'apres saint Jacques," *La Maison-Dieu* 113 (1973) 50–56. See also Leonel Mitchell, *Baptismal Anointing* (Notre Dame, Ind.: University of Notre Dame Press, 1978).

10. M.J. Lagrange, *Evangile selon saint Marc* (Paris, 1947) 154f.

11. H. Denzinger and A. Schönmetzer (eds.), *Enchiridion Symbolorum*, no. 1695, as translated in *The Christian Faith*, J. Neuner and J. Dupuis (Westminster, Md.: Christian Classics, revised 1975) 441–42.

12. Bo Reicke, *The Epistles of James, Peter, and Jude*. Anchor Bible (Garden City, N.Y.: Doubleday, 1964) 56–63. See also Martin Dibelius, *James. A Commentary on the Epistle of James.* Hermeneia (Philadelphia: Fortress Press, 1976) 251–56; Franz Mussner, *Der Jakobusbrief*, Herder Theologischer Kommentar zum Neuen Testament XIII/I (Freiburg: Herder, 1964) 218–29; Thomas W. Leahy, "The Epistle of James," in *The Jerome Biblical Commentary* (Englewood Cliffs, N.J.: Prentice-Hall, 1968) II, 376–77; Sophie Laws, *A Commentary on the Epistle of James*. Harper's New Testament Commentaries (San Francisco: Harper & Row, 1980) 224–35; James Anderson, *The Epistle of James*. The New International Commentary on the New Testament (Grand Rapids, Mich.: Eerdmans, 1976) 196–200; Richard Kugelman, *James and Jude*. New Testament Message, vol. 19 (Wilmington, Del.: Michael Glazier, 1980) 63–69.

13. Raymond Brown, "Episcopé and Episkopos: The New Testament Evidence," *Theological Studies* 41 (1980) 322–38.

14. *On Leviticus*, Hom. 2 (Griechische Christliche Schriftsteller der Ersten drei Jahrhunderts 29, 295ff).

15. Origen, *On Leviticus*, Hom. 2; John Chrysostom, *On the Priesthood* 3.6 (PG 48, 643f); Bede the Venerable, *On the*

Epistle of James 5 (PL 93, 39f); Fourteenth Session of the Council of Trent, Denzinger-Schönmetzer no. 1679.

16. Antoine Chavasse, *Etude sur l'onction des infirmes dans l'église latine du IIIe au XIe siecle*. Vol. I: *Au IIIe siecle a la reforme carolingienne* (Lyon, 1942). The insights of Chavasse's unpublished second volume are available to us through Placid Murray, "The Liturgical History of Extreme Unction," *The Furrow* 11 (1960) 572–93.

17. Gregory Dix (ed.), *The Apostolic Tradition* (London: SPCK, 1968), V, p. 10.

18. Paul F. Palmer (ed.), *Sacraments and Forgiveness*. Sources of Christian Theology II. (Westminster, Md.: Newman Press, 1959) 280.

19. Palmer, *Sacraments and Forgiveness* 288.

20. Palmer, *Sacraments and Forgiveness* 283, 284. Although the word "chrism" is used, it would probably be more accurate to speak of "the holy oil of chrismation" (i.e., of anointing generally).

21. Sermon 279, 5 (PL 39, 2273), reprinted in Palmer, *Sacraments and Forgiveness* 285.

22. Sermon 19, 5, reprinted in Henry G. J. Beck, *The Pastoral Care of Souls in South-East France During the Sixth Century*, Analecta Gregoriana (Rome, 1950) 244, 245.

23. *On Correctness of Catholic Conduct* 5 (PL 40, 1172f), reprinted in Palmer, *Sacraments and Forgiveness* 285, 286.

24. Palmer, *Sacraments and Forgiveness* 286, 287.

25. Chavasse, *Etude* 141, 142.

26. Chavasse, *Etude* 143, 144.

27. Chavasse, *Etude* 163–202. Chavasse's valuable research is more readily available in Claude Ortemann, *Le sacrement des malades* (Paris: Editions du Chalet, 1971) 21–70.

28. Dix, *Apostolic Tradition* vol. 15, p. 22: "If anyone among the laity appears to have received a gift of healing by a revelation, hands shall not be laid upon him, because the matter is manifest."

29.   Adolf Knauber, *Pastoral Theology of the Anointing of the Sick* (Collegeville, Minn.: Liturgical Press, 1975) 16A, 17A. This is the best single essay on the history and theology of anointing of the sick.

30.   PL 78, 231–36. See H. B. Porter, "The Origin of the Medieval Rite for Anointing the Sick or Dying," *Journal of Theological Studies* 7 (1956) 211–25.

31.   As translated and reprinted in Palmer, *Sacraments and Forgiveness* 293–96.

32.   Mansi XIV, 104, as translated in Palmer, *Sacraments and Forgiveness* 290–91.

33.   Mansi XIV, 932f, as translated in Palmer, *Sacraments and Forgiveness* 292.

34.   Antoine Chavasse, "Prieres pour les malades et onction sacramentelle," *L'Eglise en prière,* ed. A. G. Martimort (Paris: Desclee, 3rd rev. ed. 1965) 596–612. See also Roger Béraudy, "Le sacrament des malades," *Nouvelle Revue Theologique* 96 (1974) 600–34.

35.   Peter Browe, "Die letzte Ölung in der abendländischen Kirche des Mittelalters," *Zeitschrift für katholische Theologie* 55 (1931) 515–61.

36.   *De sacramentis* 2, 15, 2 (PL 176, 577f), as translated in Paul F. Palmer, "The Purpose of Anointing the Sick: A Reappraisal, " *Theological Studies* 19 (1958) 326. Fr. Palmer was one of the first English-speaking theologians to advance the restoration of anointing as a sacrament of the sick.

37.   *Sententiae;* as cited and translated by Palmer, "The Purpose of Anointing the Sick" 327.

38.   Palmer, "Anointing" 327.

39.   *Summa aurea in 4 Sent.;* Palmer "Anointing" 327.

40.   *Epitome* (PL 178, 1744); Palmer, "Anointing" 328.

41.   *Summa sententiarum* (PL 176, 153); Palmer, "Anointing" 328.

42.   *De septem sacramentis;* Palmer "Anointing" 328.

43. *Opera omnia* 1, 2: *De sacramentis in generali*, Palmer, "Anointing" 331.

44. Suppl., q. 30, a. 1; Palmer, "Anointing" 333.

45. *Breviloquium* 6, 11; Palmer "Anointing" 334.

46. *In 4 Sent. (Opus Parisiense)* d. 23. q. unica; Palmer, "Anointing" 335.

47. Denzinger-Schönmetzer no. 1324. Nuener and Dupuis, *The Christian Faith* 430.

48. *De captivitate Babylonica ecclesiae praeludium*, D. Martin *Luthers Werke*, Kritische Gesamtauggabe VI (Weimar, 1888) 567–71.

49. *WA Briefwechsel*, Bd. 11, Nr. 4120, 111–12.

50. *Joannis Calvini Opera Selecta*, ed. Peter Barth and Wm. Niesel, vol. 5 (Munich: Chr. Kaiser, 2nd rev. ed. 1962) 452–55.

51. Denzinger-Schönmetzer nos. 1695–1999. Neuner and Dupuis, *The Christian Faith* 441–43.

52. Denzinger-Schönmetzer nos. 1716–19. See Neuner and Dupuis, *The Christian Faith* 446–47.

53. Denzinger-Schönmetzer no. 1698. See Andre Duval, "L'extrême-onction au concil de Trente. Sacrement des mourants ou sacrement des malades," *La Maison-Dieu* 101 (1970) 127–72, esp. 171–72.

54. *Catechism of the Council of Trent* 2, 269, as cited in Palmer, "Anointing" 339.

55. *Catechism*, 2, 272; Palmer, "Anointing" 339.

56. *Acta Apostolicae Sedis* 13, 345; Palmer, "Anointing" 340.

57. AAS 15, 105; Palmer, "Anointing" 341.

58. Flannery, *Constitution on the Sacred Liturgy* 22.

59. Flannery, *Constitution on the Sacred Liturgy* 22.

60. Jacobus Goar (ed.) *Euchologion sive Rituale Graecorum* (Venice: 2nd ed., 1730) 322–57. See also Theophilus Spacil, "Doctrina Theologiae orientis separate de sacra infirmorum

unctione," *Orientalia Christiana* 24 (1931) 45–259. For an English translation, see *Service Book of the Holy Orthodox-Catholic Apostolic Church*, ed. Isabel Hapgood (Englewood, N.J.: 5th ed. 1975) 332–359.

61. Charles W. Gusmer, *The Ministry of Healing in the Church of England, An Ecumenical-Liturgical Study* (London: Alcuin Club, 1974); "Anointing of the Sick in the Church of England," *Worship* 45 (1971) 262–72.

62. *The Book of Common Prayer* (New York: Church Hymnal Corporation and The Seabury Press, 1979) 308. All the services necessary in ministering to the sick have been further compiled and edited by Leo Malania in a handy vade mecum entitled *Ministry to the Sick* (New York: The Church Hymnal Corporation, 1977).

63. Malania, *Ministry to the Sick* (New York: Church Hymnal Corporation, 1977).

64. *Occasional Services.* A companion to the *Lutheran Book of Worship* (Minneapolis: Augsburg, 1982) 94.

65. *Occasional Services* 101.

The Reforms

Chapter Two

The Reformed Rites for the Sick

In November 1969, after four years of preparation in committees, the initial draft of texts and rites for the sick was presented to the Congregation for Divine Worship, where it was further refined in November 1970.[1] In the meantime, individual dioceses in France and the United States conducted local experiments based on the original schema. The communal services of anointing at Lourdes, for example, met with great success.[2] In 1971, the International Committee on English in the Liturgy translated these provisional rites for the sick. In November of the same year, the American bishops petitioned Rome for a collective indult to use the ICEL provisional rites, a permission that was denied because the publication of the finalized Latin version for the Roman Communion was imminent. The official Vatican typical edition was promulgated on December 7, 1972, together with an accompanying apostolic constitution, *Sacram Unctionem Infirmorum*, from Paul VI dated November 30, 1972.

It is of interest to note the progress in revision made during the short months from the 1970 draft to the official text of 1972. The 1970 draft consisted of five chapters:

   I   Visitation and Communion of the Sick
  II Rite of Anointing a Sick Person at the beginning of the Danger of Death
 III Viaticum

Not included was Confirmation of a Person in Danger
of Death, presumably because the revision of the
confirmation rite had not yet been completed. The
Rites for the Commendation of the Dying were also
absent. There had been some concern about including
the rites for the dying with anointing, lest the
confusion of the two sacramental ministrations be
further perpetuated. The 1970 draft still retained the
"prudent or probable judgment about the danger of
death" as specified by Pius XI. The anointing was also
not to be repeated within the same illness, "but only if
a new sickness is involved or when the sickness lasts a
long time and the patient has shown some
improvement."[3] The description of the proper grace of
the sacrament was not yet as developed as it would be
in paragraph 6 of the final version. In these instances,
the finalized typical edition of 1972 represents a
considerable improvement over the 1970 draft with
one exception, the blessing of the oil within the rite.
The 1970 version, while assuming the blessing of the
oil of the sick by the bishop at the Chrism Mass, was
more indulgent:

"It [the oil] can be blessed by a priest in case of
necessity, when circumstances indicate that this
blessing may instruct or comfort the sick person and
others who are with him, or when the sacrament is
administered during Mass."[4]

Perhaps the memory of the first 800 years of anointing
with the strong insistence on the episcopal blessing of
oil led to the restriction of blessing by a priest to cases
of "true necessity."[5]

Taking into account the most recent ICEL changes in
the final version as outlined in the introduction to this

book, the most striking characteristic of *Pastoral Care of the Sick: Rites of Anointing and Viaticum* is its overall pastoral thrust, as the title of the rite indicates. The delineation of "Offices and Ministries" widens the earlier sacramental categories of priest/minister and subject/recipient. [6] There is the totally new provision for communal anointings, which admit of variation in the rite as carried out in a sickroom with family and friends and as celebrated in a parochial or diocesan liturgy. Another general feature is the clearer distinction between rites for the sick (Part I) and rites for the dying (Part II). The ritual begins with the normal ministry to the sick as found in chaper 1, Visits to the Sick, and is continued in the subsequent three chapters: Visits to a Sick Child (chap. 2), Communion of the Sick (chap. 3), and Anointing of the Sick (chap. 4). [7]

PASTORAL CARE OF THE SICK

For reasons of comparison it might be well to recall what provisions were made for visiting the sick in the *Rituale Romanum* of 1614. In view of the former Title VI, Extreme Unction, Chapter IV on the visitation and care of the sick from the post-Tridentive ritual comes as a pleasant surprise. Inasmuch as the pastoral exhortations were not included in the American *Collectio Rituum* of 1964, it might be useful to summarize these briefly.

The parish priest is to be available to visit sick parishioners and expects to be informed of their illness. He should keep a register of the sick. If legitimately impeded, he may seek out other priests and lay people to help him with this ministry. He should visit the sick with the spirit of a true priest. Although he has a responsibility to provide charity and help to the poor and destitute through alms or special collections, his primary concern is the spiritual good of the sick. In this he is to approach the sick with a sense of his own mission, and with a spiritual understanding of sickness and the value of redemptive suffering. He is to lead the sick person gently to the sacrament of penance. He may have to warn against treatment or remedies that are morally wrong. As the danger of death threatens, nothing should obscure the salvation of the soul or delay communion. If the sick person is not yet willing to confess his or her sins, the priest is to exhort the person continually by appealing to divine mercy and by public and private prayers. The priest is to provide the correct remedy to temptations and any false ideas the sick person may have. Nonverbal symbols are important: the images of Christ crucified, Mary, and the saints before one's eyes; the use of holy water; and so on. The priest is to recite prayers with the sick: versicles from psalms, the Lord's Prayer, the Hail Mary, the Creed. He may read the passion of the Lord, tell of the witness and examples of saints, or speak of the joys of heaven. The sick person should be consoled with the knowledge that the priest and parishioners are praying for him or her. The priest is to encourage the ailing Christian to settle his or her temporal affairs by making a will. Should the patient begin to recover, he or she should make the sickness a starting point for a better life by first of all going to church to thank God and to receive communion.[8]

The *Rituale Romanum* of 1614 also contained an elaborate office for visiting the sick. The introduction included the greeting of peace, the sprinkling of the room, one of four penitential psalms or Psalm 90, versicles and responses, three collects, the blessing, and sprinkling of the sick with holy water. From here five formats of a liturgy of the word were presented from which the priest could pick and choose. The basic pattern is a psalm, followed by a gospel reading, and concluded by a prayer. The suggested psalms are Psalms 6, 15, 19, 85, and 90. The gospel pericopes are

Matthew 8:5–13 (centurion's servant), Mark 16:14–18 (missionary mandate), Luke 4:38–40 (Peter's mother-in-law and the healing of the sick), John 5:1–14 (pool at Bethsaida), and John 1:1–14 (prologue). The fifth and concluding format provided for the laying on of hands and a final blessing and sprinkling with holy water.[9]

The American *Collectio Rituum* of 1964, considered a kind of appendix to the *Rituale Romanum*, emulated and simplified this pattern of service. Three different formats were provided in the Visitation and Care of the Sick:

Greeting of Peace
Sprinkling of Sick Person, Bed, and Room with Holy
    Water

I	II	III
Psalm 90	Psalm 15	Psalm 50
Mt 8:5–13	Mk 16:14–18	Jn 1:1–14
Lord have mercy	Our Father,	"Almighty,
"Grant, O Lord	versicle, and	everlasting
God, to your	response:	God, look
servant lasting	"God of	with pity upon
health of soul	heavenly	your servant
and body. . . ."	power, by	who is sick. . . ."
	your word you	
	drive away all	
	weakness and	
	sickness. . . ."	

Antiphon: "They shall lay hands upon the sick and
    they shall recover." (without any rubric for the
    imposition of hands)[10]
Concluding Blessing

To sum up, the Roman Communion's ritual provisions for visiting and caring for the sick are one of the brighter moments in its tradition of pastoral ministry.

A keen pastoral sensitivity permeates the directions given the priest on how to minister to the needs of the infirm. A strong emphasis is placed on sacramental confession and preparation for the life to come, but the possibility of the recovery of health is not excluded, in which case the restored person is to treat this blessing as a conversion experience for which he or she is to give thanks to God, a provision retained in the *Pastoral Care of the Sick* (no. 40C). The liturgical services for visitation, although lengthy when used in their entirety, are thoroughly scriptural in content, imbued with a feel for the importance of nonverbal communication with the ill (sprinkling, laying on of hands), and designed to meet the religious affections of the sick by instilling in them a greater trust in the Lord, who is their Savior and Healer.

In the Introduction to Part I, *Pastoral Care of the Sick*, however, one detects a subtle shift in the ecclesiology of pastoral ministry. In comparison to the *Rituale Romanum* of 1614, where the care of the sick was almost exclusively the pastor's responsibility, number 43 of the new rite describes the ministry to the sick as one involving the entire Christian community:

"This ministry is the common responsibility of all Christians, who should visit the sick, remember them in prayer, and celebrate the sacraments with them."

The sick are also to be remembered in the general intercessions at Sunday Mass, as well as during morning and evening prayer of the Liturgy of the Hours.

Number 44 highlights the facilitating and animating ministry of the priest within the Body of Christ, which coordinates this ministry to the sick. As the priest prepares the sick for the sacraments of penance, the eucharist, and the anointing, it is especially helpful if he can engage the sick person and family in prayer together. The priest is assisted by deacons and "other ministers of the eucharist" (acolytes and special eucharistic ministers), terms that are used advisedly throughout the rite. For example, there are services at which these ministers may preside: Visits to the Sick, Visits to a Sick Child, and Communion of the Sick—three of the four ministrations treated in Part I. This is another indication of the expansion of ministries called for by the "Offices and Ministries for the Sick."

The pastoral care of the sick is to be adapted to the nature and duration of the illness. A short-term illness that looks to the recovery of health requires a "more intensive ministry," but a long-term illness possibly culminating in death calls for a "more extensive ministry" (no. 45).

The Introduction continues with more specific advice concerning particular ministrations taken up in the subsequent individual chapters: Visits to the Sick, Visits to a Sick Child, Communion of the Sick, and Anointing of the Sick.

VISITS TO THE SICK (CHAPTER 1)
"Those who visit the sick should help them to pray, sharing with them the word of God proclaimed in the assembly from which their sickness has separated them. As the occasion permits, prayer drawn from the psalms or from other prayers or litanies may be added to the word of God. Care should be taken to prepare for a future visit during which the sick will receive the eucharist" (no. 46).

The pattern of prayer adopted for visiting the sick is the following:

Reading

Acts 3:1–10: "In the name of Jesus and the power of his Church there is salvation—even liberation from sickness."

or:

Acts 8:14–17: "Jesus fulfills the prophetic figure of the servant of God taking upon himself and relieving the suffering of God's people."

Response: Psalm 102 or Psalm 27

Lord's Prayer

Concluding Prayer (3 options)

Blessing (2 options)

The order is flexible. The minister may add some comments to help interiorize the meaning of scripture. The blessing concludes with the laying on of hands by the priest; other ministers may trace the sign of the cross on the forehead of the sick. The sick person may help plan the visit; he or she should be encouraged to pray when alone.

Lest this model format of prayer become overused, three other sources for prayer material are suggested: (1) sources contained in Part III of the rite, *Readings, Responses, and Verses from Sacred Scripture*; (2) the readings from the Lectionary, especially on Sundays; (3) psalms—many of which are so appropriate to use with the sick, litanies, and other devotional forms. In my opinion, the second source would be particularly apt for long-term illnesses, in which one could tire of a steady diet of readings on the mystery of suffering, and might wish to share in the readings of the Sunday eucharistic assembly.

The sick person is urged to offer his or her sufferings in union with Christ in prayer for the Church and for the world with intentions reminiscent of the sequence of the general intercessions: "for peace in the world; for a deepening of the life of the Spirit in the local Church; for the pope and the bishops; for people suffering in a particular disaster" (no. 56). One further step would be to transform these unspoken intentions into intercessions prayed within the rite of visitation.

All this brings us to a judgment of the value of providing a structured service for visiting the sick. As we have seen, the old *Rituale Romanum* did; the Latin typical edition and the ICEL provisional rite (Green Book) did not. Although a handy and flexible format may often be helpful, especially when several people are gathered around the sickbed, there may be occasions when a less formal and more spontaneous manner of prayer would be desirable.

VISITS TO A SICK CHILD (CHAPTER 2)
The same pattern of prayer is suggested for visiting sick children, although a greater sense of informality is encouraged. The minister is to establish "a friendly and easy relationship with the child" so as to win confidence. The minister should also help children appreciate their special place in the eyes of God, and if possible, the value of redemptive suffering for the salvation of the world.

The readings are handpicked for children, with a particular preference for Mark's gospel:

Mark 9:33–37: "Jesus proposes the child as the ideal of those who would enter the kingdom."
Mark 10:13–16: "Jesus welcomes the children and lays hands on them."
Mark 5:21–23, 35–43: "Jesus raises the daughter of Jairus and gives her back to her parents."
Mark 9:14–27: "Jesus cures a boy and gives him back to his father."
Luke 7:11–15: "Jesus raises a young man, the only son of his mother, and gives him back to her."

John 4:46–53: "Jesus gives his second sign by healing an official's son."

Other stories relating Jesus' healing ministry may also be told; a children's version of scripture could help facilitate this proclamation.

The responsory is a simple one-line verse that is repeated: "Jesus come to me," or "Jesus put your hand on me," or "Jesus bless me." After the Lord's prayer, the concluding prayers (choice of two) are adapted to the comprehension of children:

"God of love,
ever caring,
ever strong,
stand by us in our time of need.
Watch over your child N. who is sick,
look after him/her in every danger,
and grant him/her your healing and peace" (no. 69 A).

In addition to the laying on of hands (priest) and the signing of the cross (ministers), others present are invited to trace the sign of the cross on the forehead when this would appear to be opportune.

The child should also be communicated regularly, and possibly even be anointed. In case of serious illness in a child who has not yet been fully initiated, the priest should discuss with the parents the possibility of celebrating any or all of the sacraments of Christian initiation (baptism, confirmation, first eucharist).

Some further pastoral reflections on visiting sick persons, adults and children, follow. Most important of all is a sense of intentionality about what should happen during a visit to the sick. There is a difference between a social conversation and a pastoral visit.

Social Conversation	Pastoral Conversation
1. External subjects: weather, world events, local events	1. The person
2. Maintaining a congenial atmosphere	2. Accepting tension areas
3. Comfort through avoiding	3. Comfort through facing
4. Sharing stories: experiences, mutual trading	4. Helping person share himself or herself
5. Being pleasant, positive	5. Being understanding, empathetic
6. What should be	6. What is (as step to what should be)
7. Generalizing, universalizing: what they say, what people do	7. Being specific: what you do, think, feel
8. Being helpful by entertaining	8. Being helpful by intimate sharing
9. Religion: differences between churches, services, ministers	9. God: my and your relationship to God
10. People in general	10. Significant relationships of the person. [11]

Attention should also be given to the nonverbal features of communication in being present to the sick. The pastoral minister should face the person squarely: "I am available to you." An open posture without the defensive crossed arms or legs reinforces this openness of communication. Good eye contact and a feeling of relative relaxation also serve to put the patient more at ease. Responsive listening by the priest without a fear of silence also helps one to unburden oneself and to tell one's story. In this context, the story of stories, the good news of Jesus Christ, can be shared and the Christian prepared for any sacramental engagement needed. [12]

COMMUNION OF THE SICK (CHAPTER 3)

The Introduction to Part I, *Pastoral Care of the Sick*, makes it quite clear that the most important visits to the sick are those in which sacramental communion is received. It also gives crucial ecclesial reason why:

"Because the sick are prevented from celebrating the eucharist with the rest of the community, the most important visits are those during which they receive holy communion. In receiving the body and blood of Christ, the sick are united sacramentally to the Lord and are reunited with the eucharistic community from which illness has separated them" (no. 51). [13]

Two rites for communion are given: a fuller service in the context of a liturgy of the word, and a shorter service for the more restrictive environment of health-care institutions.

Priests are to provide the sick and infirm with the "opportunity to receive the eucharist frequently, even daily, especially during the Easter season" (no. 72). Those who take care of the sick may also be communicated. Once again, this provision is not for the sake of sheer convenience, but is meant to stress that the grace of communion is union with the whole Body of Christ, head and members, for the eucharist is the sacrament of Church unity. Sufficient ministers of communion should be formed and prepared for this ministry, and the service should be planned. The link with the Sunday eucharistic assembly can be emphasized by remembering the sick in the general intercessions and by taking communion to them from the parish eucharistic celebration on the Lord's Day. "For the sick the reception of communion is not only a privilege but also a sign of support and concern shown by the Christian community for its members who are ill" (no. 73). The eucharistic ministers might be publicly dismissed from the assembly after communion in order to visit the sick. They could bring along a copy of the parish bulletin and share with the shut-ins some of the highlights of the homily.

As before, the usual guidelines promoting reverence remain. The sacrament is conveyed in a pyx or "small closed container." A table covered with linen cloth is to be prepared, together with lighted candles, and where customary, a vessel of holy water. Sick people unable to take solid food may receive communion under the form of wine. The possibility for communion under both kinds is presumed. Lest a funeral atmosphere of gloom prevail, the rite happily adds: "Care should be taken to make the occasion special and joyful" (no. 74). The priest is to offer opportunities for the sacrament of penance and, when possible, occasionally celebrate Mass in the home of the sick together with their families and friends.

Communion in Ordinary Circumstances
In the *Rituale Romanum* of 1614 and the American *Collectio Rituum* of 1964, the communion of the sick was almost inextricably bound up with viaticum, the result being that neither ministration was accurately perceived. [14] The rite of communion of the sick is now supplied with a liturgical format all its own.

The structure of the rite is as follows:

Introductory Rites
   Greeting
   Sprinkling with Holy Water
   Penitential Rite

Liturgy of the Word
  Reading
  Response
  General Intercessions
Liturgy of Holy Communion
  Lord's Prayer
  Communion
  Silent Prayer
  Prayer after Communion
Concluding Rite
  Blessing

Four manners of greeting are provided for the minister, be this a priest, deacon, or eucharistic minister. The optional sprinkling with holy water has taken on a more overtly baptismal symbolism in keeping with the use of water in other liturgical revisions, such as at Mass and at funerals. A new antiphon to accompany the sprinkling has been created: "Like a stream in parched land, may the grace of the Lord refresh our lives" (no. 82B). The penitential rite, if there is no sacramental confession, parallels the order to Mass. The inclusion of a liturgy of the word has restored the traditional sequence word-action. Moreover, the word of God attempts to ensure that sacramental encounters be not only signs of grace, but also signs of lively faith. All five pericopes provided are from John's gospel; additional scripture can be drawn from the rich treasure trove of Part III, *Readings, Responses, and Verses from Sacred Scripture,* as well as from the Lectionary. A brief period of silence may follow the reading from scripture; the minister may also give a brief explanation of the reading. Provision is made for general intercessions, although no specific model is given. The liturgy of holy communion likewise corresponds to the revised order of Mass, beginning with the Lord's prayer and concluding with a prayer after communion, all of which speak to the effects of the eucharist: "you have called us to share the one bread and the one cup"; "we thank you for the nourishment you give us through your holy gift"; "may the body and blood of Christ your Son be . . . a lasting remedy for body and soul" (no. 90). Priests and deacons conclude the rite with one of two solemn blessings provided, or by making a sign of the cross with the Blessed Sacrament if any remains; other ministers conclude by making the sign of the cross on themselves while saying a simple blessing.

Communion in a Hospital or Institution
Terse directives describe the sharing of the eucharist in a hospital setting. Lest the rite of communion be reduced to an unacceptable minimum, several alternatives are open.

For example, the patients may be gathered together in groups whenever possible; additional ministers of communion could assist with the distribution or scripture readings, and other elements may be absorbed from the full rite for communion (no. 78).

The structure of the rite itself is simplified thus:

Introductory Rite
    Antiphon
Liturgy of Holy Communion
    Greeting
    Lord's Prayer
    Communion
Concluding Prayer

The ministration begins with a choice of one of three eucharistic antiphons (Thomas Aquinas's *Sacrum convivium,* and two additions) in the church, the hospital chapel, or in the first sickroom to be visited. The minister may be accompanied by someone carrying a candle. The liturgy of holy communion takes place in each of the individual rooms. In addition to possible scripture readings from the fuller rite, the Lord's prayer is encouraged whenever possible. The showing of the eucharistic bread is accompanied by the newly composed words:

"This is the Lamb of God
who takes away the sins of the world.
Happy are those who hunger and thirst,
for they shall be satisfied" (no. 95A).

The concluding prayer is prayed in the church, hospital chapel, or the last room visited. Unlike the fuller rite, there is no final blessing.

The proper time and manner of communion in a hospital or institution has long been a pastoral concern. The best time would seem to be when the hospital is least busy and the patient is most likely to be in the room. The minister of communion may often feel like a nurse bringing some tablets or pills for the sick to swallow. Hence, every effort should be made to see that this "sacred medicine" of the sacrament of the Lord's body and blood is communicated in an atmosphere of faith and prayer. A good general rule is always to inculcate a sense of reverence, reverence for the sacrament and reverence for the sick person whose eucharistic communion will draw him or her ever more deeply into the Body of Christ.

ANOINTING OF THE SICK (CHAPTER 4)
The most far-reaching reforms of the anointing rite are its unambiguous designation as a sacrament of the sick, the change in the central sacramental sign, and its new liturgical shape.

Sacrament of the Sick
"The sacrament of anointing is the proper sacrament for those Christians whose health is seriously impaired by sickness or old age" (no. 97). Nowhere in the ritual

are the misleading designations "extreme unction" or "last rites" to be found. One theologian commenting on this development praises the name because, in accord with James 5:14–15, it mentions the recipient. On the debit side, however, the name obscures the prayer of faith to which James subordinates the anointing. In this regard the term "prayer oil" (*euchelaion*) from the Eastern Church recommends itself as containing both elements of prayer and oil, but it does not mention the recipient of the sacrament. Perhaps the most accurate title for this sacrament would be "prayer of anointing the sick and infirm with oil." [15]

The recipient of the sacrament is a sick person "whose health is seriously impaired by sickness or old age" (no. 8). The faithful should be anointed as soon as there is a prudent judgment that the sickness is serious. Examples are spelled out and these will occupy us later on in this chapter. In comparison with the compromise of paragraph 73 of the *Constitution on the Sacred Liturgy* and the draft of 1970, these advances regarding the name of the sacrament and the condition for its reception point out the remarkable recovery of the primitive tradition in the evolving history of this sacrament for the sick and infirm. If the sacramental teaching of the Church is a classic instance of the evolution of doctrine, this phenomenon is especially verified by the anointing of the sick in the years since the Second Vatican Council. As we shall see later, the evolution continues.

Sacramental Sign
The sacrament still requires olive oil, although plant or vegetable oil will do where olive oil is difficult to obtain (no. 20). The ancient prayer of blessing, the *Emitte* from the Gelasian and Gregorian sacramentaries, is substantially the same, although rephrased with the

removal of the reference to the anointing of "priests, kings, prophets, and martyrs," which goes back to Hippolytus in the third century. The bishop continues to bless the oil of the sick, together with the oil of catechumens and sacred chrism, at the diocesan liturgy of the Chrism Mass on or near Holy Thursday, but priests may bless the oil in cases of necessity. Perhaps a communal anointing when additional blessed oil is needed would be one such occasion. For this reason the revised Roman *Emitte* is included within the anointing rite, as well as a litanaic prayer of thanksgiving to be said over the blessed oil.

The procedure for anointing in the 1614 *Rituale Romanum* and the English version of 1964 foresaw anointing the senses accompanied by a deprecative prayer expressive of a one-sided penitential understanding of extreme unction: "May the Lord forgive you by this holy anointing and his most loving mercy whatever sins you have committed by the use of your sight [hearing, smell, taste, power of speech, touch]". [16] The anointing of the feet could be omitted for a reasonable cause: at one time even the loins were anointed as the seat of lust. Then as now, a single anointing was sufficient in cases of necessity.

In the Apostolic Constitution, *Sacram Unctionem Infirmorum*, that accompanies the 1972 rite, Pope Paul VI introduced a change both in the liturgical action and in the liturgical word. The number of anointings is reduced to two, on the forehead and on the hands, the liturgical word being divided so that the first part is prayed while the forehead is anointed, the second part during the anointing of the hands. This represents a considerable improvement over the earlier one-sided penitential understanding with implied association of the senses with sinful actions. The ICEL *Pastoral Care of the Sick* has taken advantage of the adaptation

68

mentioned in number 24 by providing for the anointing of additional parts of the body, for example the area of pain or injury, without repeating the prayer (no. 124). As we have seen, this provision is found in the first full ritual of anointing dating from the ninth century.

Even more significant is the change in the liturgical word, the prayer of anointing that now reflects a richer and more complete theology of the sacrament. The prayer is ingeniously constructed from three sources: the *Rituale Romanum* of 1614, the Council of Trent, and the epistle of James (5:14–16). The opening words "Through this holy anointing may the Lord in his love and mercy" are taken over from the *Rituale Romanum*. "Help you with the grace of the Holy Spirit" is the phrase that the Council of Trent used to describe the possible effects of anointing. The second part of the prayer is drawn from James's injunction: "save you," "raise you up," and "frees you from sin." There was considerable controversy over the original ICEL translation of the Latin, which was rejected by Rome:

"Through this holy anointing and his great love for
   you
May the Lord help you by the power of His Holy
   Spirit. (Amen.)

"May the Lord who freed you from sin
heal you and extend his saving grace to you.
(Amen.)" [17]

Much of the conflict centered on the English rendering of the Latin *allevare* in the typical edition: "extend his saving grace to you." While the Vulgate, Trent, and Vatican II all use *alleviare* for "alleviate," "console," or "comfort," many manuscripts contain *allevare*, "to raise up," which is a more accurate Latin for the Greek *egerein.* The final English translation of the liturgical word is thus more literal and accurate:

"Through this holy anointing
may the Lord in his love and mercy help you
with the grace of the Holy Spirit. (Amen.)

"May the Lord who frees you from sin
save you and raise you up. (Amen.)" (no. 25). [18]

Liturgical Shape
The 1614 *Rituale Romanum* was a mosaic of the development of the sacrament from its original matrix of prayers for visiting the sick. The sacraments of penance and extreme unction were set between two sets of collects that spoke hopefully of healing and recovery. The revised rite of anointing has been given a new liturgical shape. Actually, three rites are provided to meet varying pastoral circumstances: Anointing outside Mass, Anointing during Mass, and Anointing in a Hospital or Institution.

Anointing outside Mass
In keeping with all the revised sacramental liturgies, the basic pattern of introduction, proclamation of the word, sacramental action, and conclusion is maintained.

Introductory Rites
    Greeting
    Sprinkling with Holy Water
    Instruction
    Penitential Rite
Liturgy of the Word
    Reading
    Response
Liturgy of Anointing
    Litany
    Laying on of Hands

Prayer over the Oil
Anointing
Prayer after Anointing
Lord's Prayer
(Liturgy of Holy Communion)
Communion
Silent Prayer
Prayer after Communion
Concluding Rite
Blessing

After the initial greeting, the optional sprinkling with holy water serves as a baptismal reminder and is provided with a new antiphon:

"The Lord is our shepherd
and leads us to streams of living water" (no. 116 A).

The opening instruction sets the context by referring to the scriptural basis of the sacrament in James 5:14–15. There follows the penitential rite as at Mass, with a new optional form C invoking the power of the paschal mystery. The sacrament of penance could also be celebrated at this time, although it would be wiser to provide an opportunity for the sick person to confess his or her sins in an unhurried and confidential manner sometime before the anointing. The readings for the liturgy of the word may be drawn from the scriptural resources of Part III, or a passage from one of the synoptic gospels may be read:

Matthew 11:25–30:   "Childlike confidence in the goodness of God will bring us the 'rest' that only Jesus can give."
Mark 2:1–2:   "Much more important than the health of our bodies is the peace and consolation of the presence of Jesus who can forgive us our sins and reconcile us with God."

Luke 7:19–23: "The healing hand of Christ is a sign of the presence of God; that same hand is extended to us in this sacrament now, to console and srengthen us."

The response consists of a brief period of silence or a brief explanation of the reading, perhaps expounding upon the extended caption provided for the gospels. This profusion of scripture is one of the happy enrichments of the rite of anointing, something totally absent in the *Rituale Romanum* of 1614. The readings serve to underscore that "through the sacrament of anointing the Church supports the sick in their struggle against illness and continues Christ's messianic work of healing" (no. 98). This new look given the old extreme unction will be even more effective when the sick person is able to participate in the sacrament with family and friends.

The celebration of the sacrament consists of three principal actions: the prayer of faith, the laying on of hands, and the anointing with oil. "This rite signifies the grace of the sacrament and confers it" (no. 5). The prayer of faith suggested by James 5 is made by the whole Church, represented at least by the priest, family, friends, and others. The prayer of faith is especially concentrated in the sacramental prayer of anointing, cast in a deprecative voice, and in the litany of intercessions. Quoting Thomas Aquinas, the rite states:

"The sick person will be saved by personal faith and the faith of the Church, which looks back to the death and resurrection of Christ, the source of the sacrament's power, and looks ahead to the future kingdom that is pledged in the sacraments" (no. 7).[19]

The litany prays for the relief and comfort of the sick, for all those dedicated to the care of the sick, and concludes with a petition that provides a transition to the laying on of hands.

The laying on of hands is no longer an afterthought appended to the prayer of exorcism, but is an integral sacramental action to be performed by the priests (presbyters) in silence. This biblical gesture with which Christ healed the sick is both a blessing for health and strength and an invocation of the Holy Spirit. Its place in the rite of anointing should be better appreciated.

After the blessing or thanksgiving prayer over the oil, priests anoint the forehead and hands, and when opportune, other parts of the body, while saying the prescribed prayer of faith. The practice of anointing the sick with oil signifies healing, strengthening, and the presence of the Spirit. The anointing may also be concelebrated in one of two ways: either one priest says the prayers and anoints while the others take the various parts and join in the laying on of hands, or in large congregations, each priest may lay hands on some of the sick and anoint them.

A choice of seven prayers after the anointing is adapted to the sick person's condition. Two are of a general nature; the others are for extreme or terminal illness, advanced age, before surgery, for a child, and for a young person. If eucharistic communion follows, it is substantially the same order as found in the Communion of the Sick. A selection of three solemn blessings concludes the anointing service.

The Anointing outside Mass is presented as the more usual mode of celebration. The rite is further adapted to meet the other pastoral situations: Anointing within Mass, where, in view of the usually larger congregation, the normative rite would be expanded and elaborated; and Anointing in a Hospital or

Institution, where for practical reasons the rite may have to be simplified and abbreviated.

Anointing within Mass
The rite of Anointing within Mass takes place in a church, or in another suitable place in the home of the sick person or in the hospital. It is especially appropriate for larger gatherings of a diocese, parish, society for the sick, or pilgrimage, that is, communal anointings with full participation including music. An opportunity for the sacrament of penance should be provided beforehand. As far as the particulars of the celebration: the priest would usually wear white vestments apart from the sacred seasons of Advent and Lent; the readings are usually drawn from the Lectionary (para. 871–875) or Part III. The Mass for the Sick is not permitted during the Easter Triduum and on most solemnities. On other important liturgical days (Sundays of Advent, Lent, Easter Season, solemnities, Ash Wednesday, weekdays of Holy Week), one of the readings from the Mass for the Sick and the special form of final blessing may be substituted.

The following is the structure of the Anointing within Mass:

Introductory Rites
   Greeting
   Reception of the Sick
   Penitential Rite
   Opening Prayer
Liturgy of the Word
Liturgy of Anointing
   Litany
   Laying on of Hands
   Prayer over the Oil
   Anointing
   Prayer after Anointing

Concluding Rites
   Blessing
   Dismissal

Special to the Anointing within Mass is the rite of reception of the sick:

"We have come together to celebrate the sacraments of anointing and eucharist. Christ is always present when we gather in his name; today we welcome him especially as physician and healer. We pray that the sick may be restored to health by the gift of his mercy and made whole in his fullness" (no. 135 A).

The anointing takes place after the liturgy of the word and before the liturgy of the eucharist, as is the case with all the other revised rites for sacraments celebrated within Mass. Newly composed are the orations: two options each for the opening prayer, prayer over the gifts, and prayer after communion and a preface and inserts for Eucharistic Prayers I, II, and III. In the words of the insert for Eucharistic Prayer III:

"Hear especially the prayers of those
   who ask for healing
in the name of your Son,
that they may never cease to praise you
for the wonders of your power" (no. 145).

Anointing in a Hospital or Institution
The pastoral introduction spells out the circumstances in which this liturgy is to be celebrated: "It is intended for those occasions when only the priest and sick person are present and the complete rite cannot be celebrated" (no. 149). The priest should inquire into the physical and spiritual condition of the sick person in order to adapt the celebration to his or her needs, when possible involving the sick person in the planning. In instances such as these, it may be necessary that the sacrament of penance take place

during the introductory rites. The wisest advice of all is that unless the condition of the sick person makes the anointing urgent, the priest may wait for a more appropriate time to celebrate the sacrament. (One thinks of anointings in emergency rooms where the sacrament is performed with about the same degree of diligence and perfunctoriness with which the necessary admissions data are filled out.) Continued pastoral care, with frequent opportunity for communion, should also be provided.

The structure of the rite is as follows:

Introductory Rites
    Greeting
    Instruction
Liturgy of Anointing
    Laying on of Hands
    Anointing
    Lord's Prayer
    Prayer after Anointing
Concluding Rite
    Blessing

Notable omissions in this ritual are the liturgy of the word and the blessing and thanksgiving over the oil, although the Jacobean prescription for anointing is incorporated into the instructional prayer. Many hospital chaplains felt frustrated with the fuller service in the 1973 Provisional Rites. The adaptation set forth in Anointing in a Hospital or Institution should meet their pastoral needs.

SPECIAL QUESTIONS
We have charted the evolution of anointing as a rite for the sick during the first 800 years to the Carolingian turning point, when its administration became restricted to priests. Through the close association with deathbed reconciliation, extreme unction took on those

features that led the scholastic theologians to call it a sacrament for the dying. Was anointing considered a sacrament during its early history, when the bishop blessed the oil that would later be applied to the sick by presbyters and lay people? This question is anachronistic, for it simply was not posed during those first centuries. It might be noted in passing, however, that Innocent I refers to the blessed oil in a nontechnical sense as a "kind of sacrament" (*genus sacramenti*), whose healing benefits could not be extended to catechumens and penitents. If the articulation of the theological systematization of seven sacraments in the twelfth century is a classic case of the development of dogma, there is nothing to prevent this evolution from continuing today. A contemporary case in point would be the sacrament of anointing itself, both in terms of the name of the sacrament and the condition for its reception. The sacrament has continued to evolve from the 1963 *Constitution on the Sacred Liturgy*, to the 1970 draft, to the 1972 Vatican typical edition, and finally to the approved ICEL *Pastoral Care of the Sick*. Today we find ourselves in a position analogous to that of the scholastics. The theologians of the twelfth and thirteenth centuries assumed extreme unction to be a sacrament of the dying, whence they sought to discern its specific sacramental reality or grace, namely, the remission of sins preparing the Christian for the beatific vision. Today we are fortunate enough to have recovered the original meaning of the anointing as a rite for the sick. But a question remains for us to answer as well: what is its specific benefit or sacramental grace? The solution is found in merging the original and primary tradition with the secondary and sacramentalist tradition of the scholastics. Three questions in particular arise: Who may anoint? Who may be anointed? What does the anointing do?

Who May Anoint?
This question has become more acute through the restoration of the permanent deacon, one of whose important responsibilities is to minister to the sick. Even more, eucharistic ministers and lay people on pastoral teams at hospitals feel an increasing sense of frustration because the ministry of anointing is withheld from them, especially at those moments when its administration would seem pastorally most fitting. The present discipline of the Roman Churches is clear. The teaching of the Council of Trent as restated in the revised rite reads: "The priest is the only proper minister of the anointing of the sick" (no. 16). [20] The selection of the term priest (*sacerdos*) is meant to be inclusive of both bishops and presbyters.

Dogmatically, the issue is far from settled. A crucial issue is the understanding of the "priest" or "presbyter." The scriptural precedent of James 5:14–15 teaches that the *presbyteroi* are not charismatic healers, but rather officeholders in the primitive Church. The tradition of the first 800 years made frequent reference to James, but there were discrepancies in interpretation. More attention was given to blessing the oil by the bishop than to the prayer over the sick conjoined with the anointing. Furthermore, there was no apparent distinction between the anointing by the presbyters or by lay people.

The Carolingian prayer, "Lord God, you have told us through the apostle James," underlining the presbyteral ministry is a living witness to the change in policy restricting the anointing to priests. The Council of Trent discussed extreme unction in 1547 and 1551. Only cursory attention was paid to the question of the minister. The Reformers maintained that the minister could be any baptized member of the priesthood of the faithful. In the forefront were the primary concerns of the sacramentality of extreme unction and the defense of the Roman practice of anointing the dying.[21]

Two possible avenues of interpretation present themselves. First, the anathemas with which the Tridentine canons conclude need not necessarily imply defined doctrine. For Trent, these anathemas of heretical positions were understood in a wider sense than would be the case today. They could at that time include doctrinal error or simply disobedience to Church authorities, that is, not infallible or irreformable statements. In the words of John Ziegler:

"It is more accurate to say that Canon Four condemns the Protestant position as being heretical in the broader sense that it represented a denial of an accepted practice of the Church, which denial was disruptive, insolent, and implied that the Church had erred."[22]

A second fruitful avenue to explore has been suggested by Paul Palmer. By "proper minister," did Trent mean that only the ordained priest has the sacramental power to anoint? The more likely understanding is that the priest alone is the *ex officio* or ordinary minister of the sacrament of the sick.[23]

There is a precedent for the extension of sacramental ministry. In the early Church, the initiation rites were presided over by a bishop; today even a non-Christian may validly baptize in emergency cases when he or she has the intention of doing what the Church does. The recent reforms of the initiation rites provide for another radical extension of ministry. For reasons of preserving the sacramental unity of baptism, confirmation, and first eucharist, the presbyter may confirm when initiating an adult or child of catechetical age, or when receiving baptized Christians into full communion.[24] As a result, the bishop has been renamed the "original minister" of confirmation. Now that the reforms of the Second Vatican Council have urged the earlier and more frequent reception of the sacrament of anointing, thus seeming to make it more available to the sick, where are sufficient ministers of anointing to be found? Here again Paul Palmer suggests that not only deacons but also lay people who care for the sick might be designated special ministers of the sacrament of the anointing of the sick.[25] All these considerations must be seen against the backdrop of a much larger problem. In view of the declining number of priests, which shows no sign of abating, the Church may be faced with the decision either to admit married people to the ordained priesthood or to extend the liturgical presidency of some sacraments to lay people. Otherwise, the alternative will be a one-sided cultic interpretation of priesthood, divested of the ministries of word and pastoral leadership, and the deprivation of the sacrament of anointing for many sick people.

Is there any solution to be found by way of ecumenical convergence among the two other Christian communions that practice anointing of the sick? The evidence is inconclusive. On the one hand, the Eastern Church reserves the administration of "prayer oil" to its presbyters. On the other hand, the Anglican Communion as represented by the American Episcopal Church permits the anointing by a deacon or lay person in emergency situations using oil blessed by a bishop or priest.

At the heart of this impasse is a conflict of two principles. According to the sacramental *tutiorist* position, the Church endorses the "safer" or surer theological opinion in matters pertaining to the salvation of its members. A particular concern to those holding this position might be the penitential understanding of anointing, which makes its presbyteral administration necessary. This penitential aspect, however, never fully clarified, has been more recently subsumed into a more holistic theology of the sacrament. On the other hand, the long-standing scholastic axiom that sacraments are for the people (*sacramenta propter homines*) would seek to make any adjustments doctrinally possible to provide the grace of anointing to ailing Christians. At stake is the "economy" (*oikonomia*) of the Church as regards the dispensation of the sacraments.[26] It would seem that there are no binding doctrinal arguments that would prohibit the extension of anointing at least to deacons, should the Church for pastoral reasons choose to do so.

This pastoral dimension is precisely where the ultimate judgment should rest. As a balance in this presentation, some pastoral concerns to be kept in mind follow. The ministerial identity of the deacon already suffers in comparison with the ordained priesthood, especially in matters sacramental, as is suggested in the often-quoted simplistic explanation: "Deacons can do everything but say Mass, hear confession, and anoint." Is the time ripe for extending the ministry of anointing to the diaconate before the overall pastoral ministry of the deacon to the sick is more firmly established? Another concern is that the diaconal anointings not dislodge the presbyteral ministry to the sick. For example, the bishop of one diocese recently had to remind his priests that the special eucharistic ministers do not dispense the priest from his pastoral responsibility to visit and bring communion to the sick. Empowering the deacon to anoint does not solve many pastoral problems when the sick Christian is first of all in need of sacramental absolution. Empowerment of the deacon as a minister of sacramental reconciliation finds little support in the tradition and would constitute a more radical reform. Finally, an unhealthy sacramental concentration or a "privatization" of the sacrament should be avoided at all costs. Sacraments cannot replace pastoral care. Anointing is only one sacrament of the sick, together with the eucharist, the sacrament of sacraments, and the sacramental action of the laying on of hands.

Who May Be Anointed?

In one sense, the substance of anointing as a sacrament of the sick has always been maintained. For example, canon 940 of the old Code of Canon Law (1917) demanded an intrinsic threat to life from sickness or old age before the sacrament could be administered. This meant that the sacrament could not be offered to soldiers marching off to imminent death or prisoners about to face execution.

The introductory section of the Recipients of the Anointing of the Sick contains some important clarifications. The recipient should be a Christian "whose health is seriously impaired by sickness or old age." This rendering of the Latin *periculose aegrotans* as "seriously" rather than "gravely," "dangerously," or "perilously" is intended to avoid an unnecessary restriction of the sacrament (no. 8n).[27] What is more, the sacrament may now be repeated during various stages in a progressive illness. Chapter 4 mentions two possibilities:

"a)   when a sick person recovers after being anointed and, at a later time, becomes sick again;
b)   when during the same illness the condition of the sick person becomes more serious" (no. 102, also no. 9).

Anointing may take place before surgery whenever a dangerous illness is the reason for surgery. The new prayer for those facing surgery, which was created for the anointing rite, underscores this provision. The U.S. Bishops' Committee on the Liturgy has issued a further clarification: "It would not seem appropriate to anoint a person who is to undergo 'routine' or cosmetic surgery, or an operation which does not have as its intention to correct a serious condition."[28]

Elderly people may be anointed if they are in a weakened condition, although no dangerous illness is present. It is clear—especially from the translation "seriously *impaired*" by sickness or old age—that old age is not so much a sickness, but rather a condition in which deteriorating health through length of years can constitute an intrinsic threat to life. Here the Bishops' Committee on the Liturgy states:

"Chronic, debilitating diseases or conditions in an old person weaken that person and place him or her in a dangerous situation. Again prudent judgment is required. An arthritic condition in one person may not be as serious or as dangerous as it is in another. Certainly there comes a point in old age when death can come at any time for any number of reasons (failure of vital functions, for example). However it is not any apparent imminence of death which would determine anointing, as it is debility (weak condition)."[29]

Children who are seriously ill may also be anointed if they have sufficient "use of reason" to be comforted by the sacrament. The earlier penitential understanding of extreme unction is the reason why the sacrament was withheld from children. They were thought to derive no benefit from a sacrament whose principal effect was the remission of sins (venial or the remnants of sin), since children were not yet capable of personal sin. The phrase "use of reason" is distinct from the more technical "age of reason" generally advanced as a criterion for first eucharist. "Use of reason" would seem to have less to do with chronological age than with a child alert enough to know in a rudimentary way that something good is happening: the healing Christ is reaching out to touch the child. One might argue about a theological inconsistency here. Admittedly sacraments are not only signs of grace but also signs of faith. Nonetheless, are they only intended for the rational and alert? Furthermore, the Western Church regularly baptizes infants; the Eastern Orthodox fully initiates them through baptism, chrismation, and first eucharist. The theological justification for infant baptism is that the children are baptized into the faith of the Church universal, local, and domestic (family). Is there not something to be said for the vicarious faith of a sick child's family? Pastoral praxis in some quarters has already gone beyond these somewhat restrictive provisions.

Priests are enjoined to "insure that the abuse of delaying the reception of the sacrament does not occur, and that the celebration takes place while the sick person is capable of active participation" (no. 99, also no. 13). Sick people who have lapsed into unconsciousness or lost the use of reason may likewise be anointed, if as Christian believers they would have requested it were they in control of their faculties. This is wise and compassionate advice; often people who recover from comas relate the anguish of being able to comprehend everything that was said to them yet being incapable of responding in a tangible way. The anointing in this case is absolute, not conditional; conditional anointing is done only when there is doubt whether the person is still alive.

The priest is not to anoint a person who has already died. Number 15 is very direct on this point. The priest is to "pray for them asking that God forgive their sins and graciously receive them into the kingdom." Only in cases where there is doubt whether the sick person has actually died may the priest administer the sacrament conditionally. One bishop has directed the pastoral practice for his diocese in such ways that when the doctor has already pronounced the person dead, the body is not to be anointed. In such instances the family becomes the immediate object of pastoral care, not the deceased. The inclusion of the ritual of Prayers for the Dead (chap. 7) should help ease these emotionally packed situations.

May the mentally or emotionally ill be anointed? A more holistic approach toward the sacrament finds expression in number 53 of *Pastoral Care:*

"Some types of mental sickness are now classified as serious. Those who are judged to have a serious mental illness and who would be strengthened by the sacrament may be anointed. The anointing may be repeated in accordance with the conditions for other kinds of serious illness."

Some rehabilitation centers for alcoholics under Catholic auspices regularly conduct communal anointings, for alcoholism is considered a disease, as drug addiction might also be. Before anointing Christians who are seriously ill with mental sickness, some consultation should be made with those entrusted with their medical care so as to ascertain whether the sacrament would truly be of benefit and consolation.

May non-Roman Christians be anointed? The answer to this question is found in the *Ecumenical Directory* of 1967, where the same principles stipulated for admission to communion would also apply here:

serious need, no minister of the person's own denomination, a spontaneous request for the anointing, a faith in harmony with the sacrament, and avoidance of scandal.[30] These are exceptional circumstances and most Catholic hospital chaplains are reluctant to move in this direction for fear of alienating ecumenical sensitivities.

May catechumens be anointed? Number 18 of the *Rite of Christian Initiation of Adults* declares that upon reception into the order of catechumens, the candidate is already considered to be within the "household of Christ," albeit not yet a faithful (*fidelis*) or communicant member.[31] For example, when two catechumens marry or a catechumen marries an unbaptized person, chapter 3 from the *Rite of Marriage* (Rite for Celebrating Marriage between a Catholic and an Unbaptized Person) is to be used; similarly, a catechumen who dies receives a Christian burial. In both marriages and funerals, however, the liturgical service is not necessarily a sacrament of the Church. All sacraments build upon baptism/initiation as a foundation. In the case of critical illness, Christian Initiation for the Dying from chapter 8 of *Pastoral Care* should be consulted. Whatever the case, the catechumen who is ill should be the beneficiary of the caring love of the Christian community through its intercessory prayer and visits. The laying on of hands, a frequent catechumenal gesture, would seem to be the appropriate sacramental rite.

A question that arises with increasing frequency at communal anointings is whether everyone may be anointed indiscriminately out of a sense of solidarity with the sick or for other reasons. Or again, what is to be said of communal services inviting everyone over 65 to partake of the sacrament? *Pastoral Care* gives a clear indication of the mind of the Church in this matter when speaking of anointing of the sick with a large congregation:

"In particular, the practice of indiscriminately anointing numbers of people on these occasions simply because they are ill or have reached advanced age is to be avoided. Only those whose health is seriously impaired by sickness or old age are proper subjects for the sacrament" (no. 108, also no. 99).

Upon reflection, it would seem wise that those to be anointed should be identified in advance and given preparatory instruction. A communion call list would be a good way to start. No other sacrament is administered indiscriminately, not baptism, confirmation, first eucharist, penance, marriage, or orders. Why then anointing of the sick? The practice of indiscriminate anointing could undercut the whole reform of the sacrament by trivializing serious sickness and reducing the anointing to the level of the blessing of throats on the feast of St. Blase.

An attentive pastoral ministry to the sick will usually dictate who should be anointed, how often to anoint, or whether some other sacramental ministration is called for. However useful it may be to note the different conditions that suggest anointing or to urge consultation with a doctor when in doubt, most important of all, it is not so much the person's medical condition that is determinative. It is rather the "religious" condition, a spiritual powerlessness, the crisis that illness represents in the life of an ailing Christian as regards communication with self, others, and God. Recall the carefully chosen words of number 8: "seriously impaired by sickness or old age." Anointing addresses this crisis situation: life with Christ in the community of the Church, which is threatened by serious illness, in short, salvation.

What Does the Anointing Do?

Before setting forth several models of approach to this question, some preliminary observations are in order. First, one could challenge the propriety of the question itself. What does any sacrament do? We have labored under a cause and effect mentality for the sacraments ever since the loss of a lively symbolic consciousness in the early Middle Ages. As a result, sacraments become things to be manipulated rather than actions symbolic of a dialogical communication with the mystery of the Triune God. This sacramental dialogue involves a transformation of our very being, our divinization that is at the same time our humanization, which in turn calls forth our response of faith and worship. The grace of the sacraments according to the medieval model may become a kind of spiritual capital to be amassed rather than the indwelling personal presence of the Father, Son, and Spirit that is expressed and intensified in every sacramental encounter. Finally, the prayer element is often reduced simply to petition, to the exclusion of the deeper affections of praise and thanksgiving. Thomas Talley describes this all too familiar mindset: "All preoccupation is with 'recipient,' 'minister,' a few 'principles'; you administer the sacrament and then you stand back and see if it works."[32]

Another consideration is the rich ambiguity of the word healing. Healing may be considered a synonym for everything God has done for us in Christ Jesus: salvation, redemption, justification, liberation, and reconciliation. One of the earliest depictions of Jesus in the synoptic gospels and in the Fathers' writings was Christ as a doctor sent to save the human race, inexorably plunged into a fallen-sickness-sin situation. The contemporary term "wholeness" is borrowed from psychology with the intention of illustrating how divine grace transforms the entire person. David Power has written:

". . . in the sacrament of the sick what is at stake is the sacramentality of sickness itself, or perhaps it would be better to say, the mystery which is revealed in the sick person who lives through this experience. In other words, the accent is not on healing, nor on forgiving, nor on preparing for death. It is on the sick person, who through this experience discovers God in a particular way and reveals this to the community."[33]

Four models of approach to discerning the specific grace of the sacrament of anointing the sick follow.

Ritual Anthropology

Sacramental liturgy is Christian religious ritual. In any ritual action, we spell out in word and action the meaning of a given experience, be this a family birthday, a graduation from school, a presidential inauguration, or an international ritual such as the opening or closing of the Olympic Games. As a result of the ritual celebration, the meaning of the experience is both framed or expressed and at the same time deepened, prolonged, and intensified. Applied to the sacraments, the primordial experience we ritualize at all times is the religious experience of the mystery of God revealed in the crucified and risen Christ. More specifically, the sacrament of anointing is a way of spelling out in word and action the meaning of serious illness as it touches upon this paschal mystery, the root metaphor of Christian existence.[34] This experience is both expressed in and transformed by the celebration of the sacrament, as the sick person finds himself or herself conformed more intimately to Christ and participating more deeply in this life-giving paschal mystery.

Liturgical Theology

Legem credendi lex statuat supplicandi: the rule of prayer constitutes the rule of belief.[35] This patristic axiom means that the primary sources for articulating a theology of a given sacrament are the words and actions of its liturgical celebration. Theology proceeds from faith and worship—orthodoxy according to its original meaning as *theologia prima*—from the very encounter with the mystery of God, a graced encounter celebrated in liturgical signs and words.

The prayers for blessing oil and its application yield a rich harvest for a theology of this sacrament intended for the sick. The blessing of oil in the revised *Emitte* Prayer is an epiclesis for healing and protection of the whole person:

"God of all consolation,
you chose and sent your Son to heal the world.
Graciously listen to our prayer of faith:
send the power of your Holy Spirit, the Consoler,
into this precious oil, this soothing ointment,
this rich gift, this fruit of the earth.

"Bless this oil and sanctify it for our use.

"Make this oil a remedy for all who are anointed
     with it;
heal them in body, in soul, and in spirit,
and deliver them from every affliction" (no. 123).

The thanksgiving prayer over the blessed oil speaks of Jesus' desire to "heal our infirmities"; the Spirit is praised for the "unfailing power" which "gives us strength in our bodily weakness" of the suffering Christian (no. 123). As we have already seen, the prayer that accompanies the actual anointing, the liturgical word, refers to the Lord's "love and mercy," "the grace of the Holy Spirit." Verbs rich in ambiguity describe its healing benefits: "frees you from sin," "save you," and "raise you up" (no. 124).

Number 6 from the Introduction, taken largely from the Council of Trent, relates the possible spiritual, psychological, and physical benefits of the anointing:

"This sacrament gives the grace of the Holy Spirit to those who are sick: by this grace the whole person is helped and saved, sustained by trust in God, and strengthened against the temptations of the Evil One and against anxiey over death. Thus the sick person is able not only to bear suffering bravely, but also to fight against it. A return to physical health may follow the reception of this sacrament if it will be beneficial to the sick person's salvation. If necessary, the sacrament also provides the sick person with the forgiveness of sins and the completion of Christian penance."[36]

A theology of anointing may be found not only in the words but also in the substance of oil used and the actions performed to apply it. Oil used as a soothing medicament for healing purposes is perhaps our easiest appropriation of this ancient symbol overladen with many meanings. Touching or caressing is a primordial symbolic action expressive of gentle, caring strength, as well as the conferral of the Holy Spirit.

Sacramental Transformation
The transformation that occurs in every sacramental encounter may be described as our humanization ("The glory of God is the human person fully alive")[37] or our divinization ("May we come to share in the divinity of Christ who humbled himself to share in our humanity.")[38] In either case, our sacramental sanctification is a trinitarian one. We are invited to share in the life of the Triune God. This participation begins with the Father, the source of the Godhead, proceeds through the Son, and is accomplished in the power of the Holy Spirit, the principle of divine perfection and realization. Our prayerful response is addressed in the Spirit through Christ to the Father. With reference to the sacrament of anointing, the will of the Father is complete wholeness of body, mind, and spirit, an intention thwarted by the obstacle of human sin and the concomitant disharmony that this

sin introduces into the cosmic order. "Through Christ" means that the ultimate healing now comes to us through participation in his paschal mystery: total restoration is possible only by passing through this same process of suffering to resurrection. The Holy Spirit, always a central focus of the *Emitte* Prayer of blessing the oil, is now happily mentioned also in the prayer of anointing. The Spirit is the first pledge of Christ's resurrection and a pledge of our own future resurrection. The Spirit enables us to pray, thus keeping our prayer God-centered and attuned to praise and thanksgiving even amid affliction, which is a hallmark of genuine Christian piety in that paschal joy exists even in the throes of suffering. The discernment of the Spirit can also be a great aid in discovering just what concrete expectations the sick person and the healing Church can look forward to.

Existential

Sickness constitutes a crisis of faith for the sick person, a disharmony and disintegration of one's whole being in the world. Serious illness thus represents a crisis of communication with self, with others, and with God. It is a crisis of communication from within, where the inner person or subject, the principle of human freedom and response, wrestles with a disordered nature. One has to contend with the spatial disability of a body which no longer symbolizes what the inner self desires or intends. This is also the temporal disability of a disconnected present: the past is quickly forgotten and the future is grasped in a confused sort of way with the result that everything collapses into an endless now. Oftentimes, the sick person is excessively self-preoccupied and turned inward. There is also a crisis of communication from without, in relationships with others. The sick person may be confined to a hospital or health-care institution, segregated from life as it is normally lived, deprived of the immediate love and support of family and friends and the meaning provided by one's work or profession. Illness with its unavoidable isolation and frequent real or imagined rejection is a desocializing experience. Finally, there is a crisis in one's relationship with God. Prayer is usually difficult. One is vividly reminded of human frailty and contingency. Has God abandoned me? Is there more than the present anguish and distress or is our life of faith a grand delusion?

This crisis of communication in all its dimensions is an ambivalent situation: it may lead to growth or grace, or it may lead to regression and sin. We are challenged to give meaning to this ambivalence. When properly disposed and received in faith, the sick Christian will normally experience some inner strengthening, some betterment, as is often observed by those who minister and those who receive the sacrament. One could say that the sick person is always healed in some way, but not necessarily cured of the disease or affliction. There is also an important aspect of resocializing: a developed pastoral ministry to the sick and the celebration of communal anointings are good ways of highlighting the acceptance by the healing community of the Church. Finally, in relation to God there is a greater trust, confidence, and surrender to a divine mystery of unconditional love who paradoxically heals through the power of the cross.

A growing number of authors would concur with the general lines of this more existential approach. Claude Ortemann sees the sacrament within the perspective of eschatological hope as a reunification of the subject to the material world according to four dimensions: (1) reconciliation with the body, (2) restoration of a sense of solidarity with the world, (3) integration of finiteness and death, and (4) integration of the temporality of life.[39] James Empereur calls anointing a vocation sacrament, a rite of passage that removes the threat and ambiguity posed by sickness and old age by allowing the sick and elderly to enter into the passage of Christ from death to life. In this way, alienation and brokenness are converted into an anticipated experience of resurrected life.[40] The words of Jennifer Glen provide an especially hopeful and consoling conclusion:

"Sickness is less halting-place than passage, provided that it be seen to open out beyond the closed present of the sickworld onto a future which imparts to it direction and therefore meaning. Through its rituals for the sick, particularly through the rites of the laying on of hands and the anointing with oil, the Christian community holds out to its sick, in symbol, its own faith that the mystery of death which confronts them in the dark corridor is not its end. It does not seal them into an eternal, hopeless present from which there is no issue. He who has been separated from his own person, from his fellow human beings, and from his conception of God by the diagnosis of illness need not despair; all that has been lost shall be restored, renewed, within the horizon of a future that is partial now in pledge that it will be absolute."[41]

NOTES

1. *Notitiae* 59 (1970) 388–89.

2. *Notitiae* 59 (1970) 22–23.

3. *Rites for the Sick* (Washington: ICEL, 1971), no. 9.

4. *Rites for the Sick*, no. 21.

5. *Pastoral Care of the Sick: Rites of Anointing and Viaticum* (Washington: ICEL, 1982), no. 21b.

6. Nos. 32–37. This new pastoral thrust is immediately evident in the General Introduction or *Praenotanda*.

7. For commentaries see special issues of *La Maison-Dieu* 113 (1973) and *Ephemerides Liturgicae* 89 (1975), as well as

Bishops' Committee on the Liturgy, *Study Text II: Anointing and the Pastoral Care of the Sick* (Washington: USCC Publications, 1973).

8. *Rituale Romanum,* tit. VI De sacramento extremae unctionis, cap. IV De visitatione et cura infirmorum, para. 1–17.

9. *Rituale Romanum,* tit. VI De sacramento extremae unctionis, cap. IV De visitatione et cura infirmorum, para. 18–26.

10. *Collectio Rituum* pro dioecesibus civitatum foederatarum americae septentrionalis (*English Ritual*) (Collegeville, 1964), "The Visitation and Care of the Sick" pp. 237–55.

11. I am grateful to Sr. Alice McCoy, O.P., for providing this contrast between a social and pastoral conversation.

12. Susan Borrelli, *With Care, Reflections of a Minister to the Sick.* (Chicago: Liturgy Training Publications, 1980).

13. See also Nathan Mitchell, *Cult and Controversy: The Worship of the Eucharist outside Mass* (New York: Pueblo, 1982) 112–16, 268ff et passim; William Belford, *Special Ministers of the Eucharist* (New York: Pueblo, 1979).

14. The English Ritual even conjoined the two ministrations: "The Rite for the Administration of Viaticum and Communion of the Sick."

15. J. Feiner, "Die Krankheit und das Sakrament des Salbungsgebetes," in *Mysterium Salutis,* V, 494–550.

16. "The Rite for Administering the Sacrament of the Anointing of the Sick," *English Ritual* 220–35.

17. *Rites for the Sick,* no. 25.

18. A. Verheul, "The Paschal Character of the Sacrament of the Sick: Exegesis of James 5:14–15 and the New Rite for the Sacrament of the Sick," *Temple of the Holy Spirit: Sickness and Death of the Christian in the Liturgy* (New York: Pueblo, 1983) 247–58. This article studies the origin of the new sacramental form or liturgical word. See also the varying vernacular translations in *Notitiae* 10 (1974) 89–91. Verheul concludes that the final English rendering is the most satisfying.

19. Citing Thomas Aquinas, *In 4 Sententiarum*, d. 1, q. 1, a. 4, quaestiuncula.

20. Citing Council of Trent, sess. 14, *De Extrema Unctione*, cap. 3 and cap. 4 (DS 1697 and 1719).

21. See A. Duval, "L'extreme-onction au Concile de Trente," *La Maison-Dieu* 101 (1970) 127–72.

22. "The Possibility of the Church Appointing the Deacon as a Minister of the Anointing of the Sick and The Council of Trent." Unpublished paper prepared for the National Conference of Diocesan Directors of the Permanent Diaconate (Winter 1976).

23. Paul F. Palmer, "Who Can Anoint the Sick?" *Worship* 48 (1974) 81–92.

24. *Rite of Confirmation*, para. 7, G.

25. Palmer, "Who Can Anoint the Sick?" 92. See also Philippe Rouillard, "Le ministère du sacrement de l'onction des malades," *Nouvelle Révue Théologique* 101 (1979) 395–402.

26. Ladislaus Orsy, "In Search of the Meaning of *Oikonomia*: Report on a Convention," *Theological Studies* 43 (1982) 312–19.

27. The footnote as originally proposed by ICEL read:

"The word *periculose* has been carefully studied and rendered as 'seriously,' rather than as 'gravely,' 'dangerously,' or 'perilously' in order to respect the development from *Sacrosanctum Concilium*, n. 73 (*incipit esse in periculo mortis*) to the Apostolic Constitution *Sacram Unctionis Infirmorum* (*periculose aegrotantibus*) and the *Ordo Unctionis, Praenotanda* n. 8. Such a rendering will serve to avoid restrictions upon the celebration or the sacrament contrary to the letter and spirit of this development. On the one hand, the sacrament may and should be given to anyone whose health is seriously impaired; on the other hand, it may not be given indiscriminately or to any person whose health is not seriously impaired."

In other words, the Congregation for Sacraments and Worship insisted on minimalizing the notion of development in discerning the proper subject of the sacrament. The impasse over the translation of *periculose* was the principal difficulty Rome had with the ICEL revision, causing a delay of over two years and forcing a confrontation with the Episcopal Board of ICEL.

28. *Newsletter* XV (March–April 1979).

29. *Newsletter* XV (March–April 1979). The Bishops' Committee on the Liturgy already addressed this issue in the earlier *Newsletter* X (March 1974).

30. *Ecumenical Directory*, Pt. I, para. 55 (*Ad Totam Ecclesiam*, May 14, 1967), Flannery p. 499.

31. See Aidan Kavanagh, *The Shape of Baptism: The Rite of Christian Initiation* (New York: Pueblo, 1978) 109–14, 129–33.

32. "Visiting, Caring for, Anointing the Sick: Reflections on Persons, Rites, and the Church," *Living Worship*, vol. 8 (September 1972), which was a summary of the June conference of the then Notre Dame Murphy Center for Liturgical Research.

33. David Power, "Let the Sick Man Call," *The Heythrop Journal* 19 (1978) 262.

34. George S. Worgul, *From Magic to Metaphor* (New York: Paulist, 1980) 184–95. I am also indebted to John Gallen for these insights from his liturgical methodology.

35. Prosper of Aquitaine, *Indiculus de Gratia Dei* 8 (PL51, 209f).

36. Council of Trent, sess. 14, *De Extrema Unctione*, prooem, and cap. 2 (DS 1694 and 1696).

37. Irenaeus of Lyon, *Adversus omnes Haereses*, IV, 19.

38. Prayer in the Sacramentary to be prayed quietly during the mixture of water and wine at the preparation of eucharistic gifts, taken from an old Roman oration.

39. Claude Ortemann, *Le sacrement des malades* 93–123. See also Francois Isambert, *Rite et efficacité symbolique* (Paris: Editions du Cerf, 1979) 115–57; Thomas Marsh, "A Theology of Anointing the Sick," *The Furrow* 29 (1978)

89–101, Bernard Sesboüé, *L'onction des malades* (Lyons: Profac, 1972).

40.   James L. Empereur, *Prophetic Anointing*. Message of the Sacraments 7. (Wilmington, Del.: Michael Glazier, 1982) 141–203.

41.   M. Jennifer Glen, "Sickness and Symbol: The Promise of the Future," *Worship* 54 (1980) 411.

Chapter Three

The Reformed Rites for the Dying

Today most people die in institutions, away from home and family. The familiar sights and sounds and smells of household and neighborhood are absent in the antiseptic and depersonalized cubicle of a hospital. Dying can be a long and complex process. At times, it can even be a misfortune to be in a superior hospital where technological excellence preserves life much longer than seems necessary. For example, pneumonia has largely ceased to be the "old man's friend" as it was in the past. Dying can also be expensive, literally wiping out a family's savings accumulated over a lifetime. Finally, a conspiracy of silence shrouds the dying process, making it difficult if not impossible for the critically ill to talk openly about impending death. For the medical practice, death constitutes a failure or loss. The dying are frequently treated to well-meaning but vacuous remarks such as "No, you'll get better" or "Keep your spirits up." This death-denying atmosphere only serves to intensify the dying person's isolation and loneliness.[1] A welcome contrast to all this is the hospice movement of caring for the dying. This medieval Christian practice has been reinaugurated by Dr. Cecily Saunders at St. Christopher's Hospice in England, and it is making a considerable impact in the United States at this time.[2]

What is going on inside the dying patient? The patient almost always knows that he or she is dying. There are many messages one intuitively hears and feels: the sound of approaching footsteps that stop before the door as the visitor pauses before entering, eyes reddened by tears, the awkwardness of conversation, avoidance by the uncomfortable medical staff. Aware of impending death, the patient almost always grieves. While there may be some overlapping or regression, Elisabeth Kübler-Ross describes the progressive stages of this anticipatory grief process: denial, anger, bargaining, depression, and acceptance. It is important for the Church to be present pastorally to the dying Christian during the progression of these stages. The first stage is denial: "No, not me." Denial is important and necessary for helping to cushion the impact of the patient's awareness of the inevitability of death. The second stage is rage and anger: "Why me?" Hostility is vented toward others who remain alive and healthy; often it is also directed against God who seems to be an arbitrary despot imposing the death sentence. Bargaining makes up the third state: "Yes me . . . but." Patients attempt to strike bargains for more time, particularly with God by promising a greater religious commitment and practice of the faith. The fourth stage is depression: "Yes, me." Mourning past and future losses, the patient grows quiet preparing for the arrival of death. Acceptance is the final stage: "My time is very close now and it's all right."[3]

As the patient approaches death, there is usually a reduction of personality, a phenomenon that accompanies physiological decline. Often there is also a reduction in religious fervor and concern; the desire for peace, quiet, and sleep usually outweighs the need for a theological explanation of the hereafter. The patient should feel safe in the arms of a mystery in which he or she can trust and remain secure. What is more, the patient always has hope. We are constantly redefining our hopes and expectations. In the beginning of the illness, the patient looks forward to being released and sent home. When this possibility appears remote, the patient longs for the day when he or she will be able to

get out of bed, to take solid food, and so on. Sigmund
Freud once commented that it is impossible for us to
visualize our own death, for deep down in our
unconscious we all believe we are immortal. This
never-flagging hope could be a "rumor of angels"
pointing to the existence of a transcendent God.[4]

THE CHURCH'S PRAYER FOR THE DYING
A number of characteristics mark the Church's
tradition of praying for the dying and the dead. The
Church prays with concrete images, never in ideas or
abstractions. These images, rooted in Christian
antiquity, are rich, diverse, and complementary. Above
all, they are steeped in a scriptural spirituality of both
Old and New Testament. For example, the
paradigmatic *Suscipe* from the Commendation of the
Dying prays for deliverance by alluding to such
scriptural figures as Noah, Abraham, Job, Moses,
Daniel, the three young men in the fiery furnace,
Susanna, David, Peter, and Paul.[5]

Death as Sleep and Eternal Repose
From the late Jewish apocalyptic book of 4 Esdras
2:34, 35 comes the *subvenite* often repeated in the
liturgies for the dying and the dead:

"Give him/her eternal rest, O Lord, and may your light
shine on him/her forever."[6]

Sleep and repose are natural images for death. "Our
friend Lazarus has fallen asleep" (Jn 11:11). Paul
speaks of those "who have fallen asleep in the Lord" (1
Cor 15:18). This image appeals convincingly to a
person whose entire being is ravaged by acute pain
and suffering, but there is a deeper religious meaning.
This repose imitates the creator God who rested on the
seventh day. Moreover, Yahweh vows that rebellious
Israel "should not enter my rest" (Ps 95:11). Hebrews
4:1–11 asserts that it is not Joshua who led the people

of God into the repose of the Lord through entry into the Promised Land, but rather that Jesus Christ alone is the one who introduces believers into the repose of God. For a Christian, eternal repose is the accomplishment of the promise of God realized in Christ (Rv 14:13). This is in marked contrast to the world of pagan antiquity and also to contemporary culture. Pagans viewed death as an eternal sleep, often in a pessimistic fashion, the dead being relegated to an afterlife in a tomb or in the lower world. Christians, on the other hand, saw death as a temporary sleep awaiting the resurrection. The word cemetery ("sleeping place") was first coined by Christians; burial inscriptions speak of "sleep," "rest," and "rest in the sleep of peace."

Death as Birth into Light, Refreshment, and Peace
Early Christians disdained the popular practice of celebrating birthdates. They preferred to celebrate the anniversary of the day of death or martyrdom, a practice observed in the Roman Martyrology and, as far as possible, in the realignment of the saints' feast days in the revised Roman Calendar. The *dies natalis* is the day of birth into eternal life, a day of true birth and resurrection for a Christian.

Death is the attainment of light. In Latin and Greek culture, light and life are hendiadys, an outlook not far removed from that of the fourth gospel: "In him was life and the life was the light of men" (Jn 1:4). Light is the natural image for joy, happiness, life, and hope. Whatever the final verdict on the authenticity of "out of the body" experiences of those thought to be clinically dead but later revived, the image of abundant light is consistently mentioned.[7]

This natural image also admits of a rich religious meaning. "God is light and in him is no darkness at all" (1 Jn 1:5). God lives in "unapproachable light" (1

Tm 6:16). God has called us "out of darkness into his own marvelous light" (1 Pt 2:9), in a passage that appears to have been part of a primitive baptismal catechesis. Jesus, himself the revelation of the Father, is the "light of the world" (Jn 8:12). In the book of Revelation 21:23, the Isaian images of light (Is 24:23; 60:1, 19) are applied to the heavenly Jerusalem. For the elect, the "Lord God will be their light, and they shall reign for ever and ever" (Rv 22:5). The Creed professes belief in the "God of Gods, light of lights." One of the earliest synonyms for baptism is "enlightenment": through baptism we are enabled to share in the light of Christ that scatters the darkness of sin and death. Eternal light is an expression of hope in the beyond. Eternal light is God in Godself.

The memento for the dead in the Roman Canon prays that they may find light, happiness, and peace. "Refreshment" might have been a more accurate rendering of the Latin *refrigerium* than "happiness." Originally, refreshment evoked the image of a green oasis surrounded by water. "Peace" is the Hebrew greeting, an image of eschatological salvation. How appropriate that these very words from the mouth of the risen Lord, "Peace be with you" (Jn 20:19; 21:26), are the very first ones addressed to the sick and the dying in the opening greeting of the revised rites: "The peace of the Lord be with you always"; "Peace be with you (this house), and with all who live here" (no. 197 A,B).

Death as a Journey to the Lord
In colloquial language, we often speak of death as a trip or journey. On his deathbed, the much-loved Pope John XXIII reassured his saddened flock that his bags were packed and he was ready to go. A comparable conception flourished in the ancient world. Egyptian eschatology foresaw a voyage into the afterlife where the deceased would be transported in the bark of the

god Re to the realm of the gods. As early as the sixth century B.C., the Greeks, and later the Romans, saw the dead taking a voyage across the river Styx through the agency of the ferryman Charon to the company of gods and heroes.

Christian antiquity seized upon this image and transformed it. Death is a journey, a migration to the Lord, setting out to live eternally with Christ, going to Christ. This image of a journey or voyage is reflected in the title of the earliest Roman orders for the sequence of rites that accompany the Christian from the dying moments to the grave: "Here begins the migration of the soul." (*Incipit de migratione animae*.) The Church is a kind of ship conveying souls to the kingdom of Christ. It is a perilous journey beset with many hazards. The first Christians echoed the conception of the Mediterranean people of their day that foes and terrifying powers awaited the soul. "Your adversary the devil prowls like a roaring lion seeking someone to devour" (1 Pet 5:8). The Church guides and protects its dying members on this journey, accompanying them as far as it can go before entrusting them to the celestial psychopomps, the angels who bear the souls of the Christian out of this life. The prayers for the dying are permeated with this vision:

"Go forth, Christian soul, from this world" (*proficiscere*).

"May holy Mary, the angels, and all the saints come to meet you as you go forth from this life" (*Commendo te*) (no. 220B).

So is this prayer after death:

"Saints of God, come to his/her aid! Come to meet him/her, angels of the Lord!" (*Subvenite*) (no. 221A).

The destination of this journey is variously described by the images of the bosom of Abraham, paradise, and the holy city of Jerusalem. Abraham is the father of believers, the first to receive the promises (Rom 4:9–25; Gal 3:6–29). He symbolizes the joy of the elect: "Your father Abraham rejoiced that he was to see my day" (Jn 8:56). The kingdom of God is described in terms of a banquet, a messianic feast prepared by the Lord for his elect. "I tell you many will come from the east and the west and sit at the table with Abraham, Isaac and Jacob in the kingdom of heaven" (Jn 8:56). The Lucan parable of Lazarus and the rich man is the clearest depiction of heavenly bliss associated with the bosom of Abraham (Lk 16:22–23): "The poor man died and was carried by the angels to Abraham's bosom." This sentiment is articulated in the prayer prayed immediately after death:

"May Christ who called you, take you to himself; may angels lead you to Abraham's side" (no. 221).

The bosom of Abraham was a frequent motif in medieval art where the patriarch is pictured holding the elect on his lap or else enveloping them in his cloak. If the need for trust and security are important for the dying, the figure of Abraham could fill this need for anyone at all familiar with the rudiments of a biblical catechesis. Abraham is the friend of God who receives us into God's dwelling. He does not function as a servile functionary. The image of the bosom of Abraham bespeaks affection, filial intimacy that is the fruit of faith. Abraham is our "grandfather" in the faith who welcomes us to our true home.

Jesus promises the repentant thief: "I say to you, today you will be with me in paradise" (Lk 22:43). Paradise is the symbol of the perfect happiness of the human family, created in the image of God and exiled from the original paradise because of sin (Gn 2, 3). Life with God, beatitude, is described by this same image used in Genesis to express the initial happiness of the human race. In terms of religious history, it is in

Revelation 22, the last book of the Bible, that paradise is rediscovered, as we cry out in the farewell chant at funerals:

"May the angels lead you into paradise,
may the martyrs come to welcome you
and take you to the holy city,
the new and eternal Jerusalem."[8]

If "paradise" appeals to the garden at the beginning of the Bible, "Jerusalem" refers to a city, the heavenly Jerusalem of the end times (Rv 22:14, 19). Both are gifts of God. Paradise is a garden planted by God. Even Jerusalem is not something we have created; the heavenly Zion, is likewise a gift. These images of paradise and Jerusalem are complementary and hence frequently juxtaposed. Paradise conjures up pictures of freshness, fantasy, freedom. Jerusalem connotes order, large throngs, assembly, a feast. Once again, the *Proficiscere*:

"May you live in peace this day, may your home be with God in Zion, with Mary, the virgin Mother of God, with Joseph, and all the angels and saints" (no. 220A).[9]

THE TRADITION OF THE VIATICUM
Ignatius of Antioch (d.c. 110), as he awaited his martyrdom, movingly tells of his desire to imitate Christ's death and resurrection as this mystery is reenacted in his own flesh: "It is better for me to die for Jesus Christ than to rule over the ends of the earth. I seek Him who died for us; I desire Him who rose for us. . . . Let me be an imitator of the passion of my God."[10] Ignatius' thoughts spontaneously drift toward the sacramentalization of this paschal mystery in the eucharist: "I desire the bread of God which is the flesh of Jesus Christ . . . and for drink I desire his blood which is incorruptible love."[11] In his letter to the Ephesians, he goes on to explain the reason for this

eucharistic yearning when he describes the sacrament as "the medicine of immortality, that antidote that results not in dying, but in living forever in Jesus Christ."[12] Similar thoughts occupy the heart of Polycarp of Smyrna (d.c. 157) when he prays his final words before martyrdom, words that reflect how traces of a primitive *berakah* or eucharistic prayer had made their way into his personal life of prayer:

"I bless thee for granting me this day and hour, that I may be numbered amongst the martyrs, to share the cup of thine Anointed and to rise again unto life everlasting both in body and soul, in the immortality of the Holy Spirit."[13]

The witness of these two early martyrs for the faith gives evidence of the eucharist as an intimate way of sharing in the mystery of Christ's death and resurrection and thus preparing for ultimate union with the Lord in death. Another source of eucharistic piety and devotion is found in the tradition of providing Christians departing this life with holy communion received as viaticum, quite literally "food for the journey."[14]

In Greek and Latin antiquity, the custom was to provide a meal for people undertaking a journey as evidenced in the Latin *viaticus*, of or pertaining to a journey, and the Greek *ephodion*, provisions for a journey. These words could also refer to a farewell meal at death, a vestige of which survived in the *refrigerium* of the early Church, a kind of picnic in a cemetery. More often, however, viaticum meant the practice of providing the fare for the voyage after life, the *obolus* or coin placed in the mouth of the deceased to pay the ferryman Charon for passage across the river Styx. In the world of Virgil and the other classical authors, viaticum was thus the money or fare for the journey.

In early ecclesiastical language, *viaticum* or *ephodion* also admitted of a variety of meanings. Viaticum could mean sustenance for the journey of life, namely the teachings of Christ and all the means of salvation. It could also refer to the journey of death: anything that gave spiritual comfort and strength to the dying and enabled them to make their journey to God, for example, the eucharist, baptism, penance, prayers, and good works. Only gradually did viaticum come to have the more specific meaning of the eucharist administered to a dying Christian.

The canonical and hagiographical literature from the third to the sixth centuries is rich and revealing. In a letter to Bishop Fabius of Antioch, Bishop Dionysius of Alexandria (265) tells the story of Serapion, an old man who lived a holy life in penance after his sin of apostasy during the Decian persecution. Approaching death in his unreconciled status, he sent his grandson to look for a presbyter. The presbyter, being ill, was unable to come but gave the boy a small portion of the eucharist to soak and let fall piece by piece into the mouth of the dying man. Serapion swallowed just a little before he breathed his last.[15] This story is set against the background of the Novatianists, an elitist sect that refused reconciliation to the *lapsi* or those fallen away; even on their deathbed they were to be refused the strength and protection of the eucharist. The first ecumenical council of Nicaea (325) felt compelled to react against this rigorism. In Canon 13, the Council legislated that "the ancient and canonical ruling is to be observed" that a dying Christian "is not to be deprived of the last and necessary provision for the journey, viaticum." It decreed further: "In general, with regard to any dying person who asks to partake of the eucharist, the bishop, after looking into the matter, will grant him to participate in the offering."[16] It appears that even if the full reconciliation accorded by the penitential discipline of the time was a closed door, another door remained open: communion by viaticum, the eucharist itself as the sacrament of reconciliation. The teaching of Nicaea was reiterated at other local councils, most notably at Orange in 441. This would also appear to be the origin of the canonical insistence regarding the importance of viaticum that finds its way into the 1917 Code of Canon Law (CIC 864), which is continued in the revised rites for the dying (no. 27).

The edifying lives of the saints likewise testify to the importance of the eucharist at the hour of death. Paulinus describes the death of St. Ambrose (397) after he received the eucharist, taking with him a good viaticum so that his soul, refreshed by this food, now enjoys the company of the saints.[17] The biographer of John Chrysostom (+407), Palladius, related how Basiliscus, the martyr-bishop of Comana, appeared to the saint in a vision to tell him that he would die the following day. Chrysostom thereupon clothed himself in festive white, received communion, and died.[18] The *Life* of Melania the Younger (+439) contains two accounts of the ministration of viaticum: "it is the custom among the Romans to have the communion of the Lord in the mouth when the souls are departing."[19] Accordingly, her uncle Volusian was communicated twice on the day of his death; Melania herself, succumbing shortly thereafter, received the eucharist three times on the day she died. In his *Dialogues*, Gregory tells of the death of St. Benedict. On the sixth day of his final illness, Benedict had himself carried to the oratory, strengthened himself with the sacrament, and breathed forth his last words of prayer.[20]

The Church's insistence on communicating the dying led to the widespread abuse of attempting to communicate the dead. The practice of placing the eucharistic bread in the mouth of the deceased and, as it appears sometimes, in the very tomb itself, was roundly condemned for the first time at the Council of Hippo (393), a plenary council in Africa, and in subsequent councils over the next three hundred years in Africa, Gaul, and the East. This abuse might be compared to a similar one that perdures today of anointing those already dead, as if God were unable to save his own apart from the confines of a sacramental system.

The emergence of the eucharist as viaticum, the sacrament of the dying, is another instance of cultural adaptation by Christian antiquity. There were, however, marked dissimilarities from pagan rites. Pagans gave "viaticum" to those already dead, to corpses; Christian viaticum is for the living. Pagans provided the dead with an inanimate coin as viaticum; Christians provided the living with life as viaticum. Christian viaticum was not intended to pay for the journey of the soul to the place of eternal rest, but was a provision for passage to eternity, being itself a pledge of eternal life.[21]

The oldest surviving Western ritual forms for the dying represent two very similar traditions: the Phillips 1667 and *Ordo Romanus* 49. The Phillips 1667, a transcription of a Gelasian Sacramentary of the eighth century containing hybrid Roman and Gallican sources, directs that:

"Before it [the soul] goes out of the body, the priest communicates with the Body and Blood, making sure that he does not die without viaticum: this is the Body of the Lord."[22]

This communion by viaticum is to take place after the reading of the passion according to John's gospel and other prayers, perhaps a witness to the primitive practice of dying with communion on the tongue. The dying Christian is prepared for death from both the table of the word and the table of the eucharist. On the other hand, *Ordo Romanus* 49, dating from the eighth century and of Roman provenance, reverses the order and lists as its first rubric the communion of the dying:

"As soon as you see death approaching, he is to be communicated from the holy sacrifice, even if he communicated the same day, because communion will be his defender and helper. For it will raise him up."[23]

So important was viaticum that the dying Christian might even take communion more than once during the same day, as did Melania and Volusian, mentioned above. The justification for this practice is rich in overtones from the bread of life discourse in the sixth chapter of John.

Until the twelfth century, communion was administered under both kinds, often with the bread intincted with the wine.[24] There were three manners of ministration: (1) the dying person could be taken to the church, as was the case with St. Benedict; (2) Mass could be celebrated at home, although this was later suppressed by Rome and only restored in our day; or, (3) as has become the most common usage, the communion rite from the reserved sacrament and without Mass took place at home. During the high Middle Ages, this service of communion often imitated the communion rite at Mass; in Celtic churches, it was even preceded by an epistle or gospel. The Lord's Prayer was the principal preparation for communion. From the eleventh century, the Our Father was gradually supplanted by the confiteor and profession of faith. For example, the twelfth-century ritual of St. Florian touchingly elicits the following act of faith from the dying Christian:

"Behold, brother, the body of our Lord Jesus Christ which we bring to you. Do you believe this is our salvation and life and resurrection. R. I believe."[25]

In the *Rituale Romanum* of 1614, viaticum was included under Title V on the eucharist as communion of the sick. Title VI, which was devoted to the sick and dying, made no mention of viaticum except for an isolated rubrical suggestion for helping the dying: following viaticum and anointing was the commendation of the soul. Not only did the arrangement represent a disorder in the original sequence of the continuous rites with extreme unction *following* viaticum, it also confused the purpose of viaticum with communion for the sick by including it within the same service.

PASTORAL CARE OF THE DYING
Not only have the liturgical reforms of the Second Vatican Council recovered *anointing* as a *sacrament for the sick,* they have also restored the proper meaning of *viaticum* as a *sacrament for the dying.* Lest an interest in promoting anointing as a sacrament for the sick mislead the faithful into believing the Church has nothing with which to comfort and strengthen its members who are departing this life, one should recall that Part II of the revision has to do with the pastoral care of the dying.

If a characteristic of the pastoral care of the sick is the Christian's struggle against illness, the ministry to the dying emphasizes trust in the Lord's promise of eternal life. The first three chapters of Part II—Viaticum, Commendation of the Dying, and Prayers for the Dead—provide for situations when time is not a pressing concern and the rites can be celebrated in a full and proper manner. Chapter 8, Rites for Exceptional Circumstances, represents pastoral adaptations to emergency situations.

Once again, the terms "priest," "deacon," and "minister" are used advisedly in the rubrics. For example, for the celebration of the sacraments of penance, anointing of the sick, and viaticum within Mass, the rite refers to "priest." When a deacon may also preside, the term "priest or deacon" is used. For the rest, the term "minister" would be inclusive of the ministry of priests, deacons, and other ministers; understood especially would be eucharistic ministers, although the term is wisely left unspecified. Just as the care of the sick is a responsibility of the entire Christian community, so also is the care of the dying:

"The Christian community has a continuing responsibility to pray for and with the person who is dying. Through its sacramental ministry to the dying the community helps Christians to embrace death in mysterious union with the crucified and risen Lord, who awaits them in the fullness of life" (no. 163).

Of special interest are the new pastoral notes concerning a dying child. In the suffering of innocent children the mystery of suffering and evil becomes most acute. The hurt and bewilderment of the parents calls forth a ministry directed both to the child and to the family. Often the faith of dying children matures rapidly, as does their anguish at the pain they perceive in their family. In addition to the ministries of priest, deacon, and other ministers, as well as the roles played by hospital personnel (doctors, nurses, aides), the Christian community might also call forth the unique ministry of those who have lost children of their own.

The stressful period when a child is dying can be turned into a time of prayer and renewal for the family and loved ones. "By conversation and brief services of readings and prayers, the minister may help the parents and family to see that their child is being called ahead of them to enter the kingdom and joy of the Lord" (no. 171). One might add that responsive listening can often be as helpful as spoken words.

When appropriate, the priest should discuss the possible preparation for and celebration of the sacraments of initiation (baptism, confirmation, eucharist) according to what is needed and called for; no age is specified. It is important that a dying Christian of any age leave this life having been fully initiated into the paschal mystery of the Lord, whom he or she will presently see face to face.

CELEBRATION OF VIATICUM (CHAPTER 5)
Number 175 from the introduction clearly indicates the mind of the Church regarding viaticum as the sacrament for the dying:

"The celebration of the eucharist as viaticum, food for the passage through death to eternal life, is the sacrament proper to the dying Christian. It is the completion and crown of the Christian life on the earth, signifying that the Christian follows the Lord to eternal glory and the banquet of the heavenly kingdom."

To this end, the sacrament of anointing should be celebrated at the beginning of serious illness, so that viaticum celebrated when death is near will be perceived as the last sacrament of Christian life, what people once supposed extreme unction to be. Priests and other ministers who care for the sick are to make every effort to see that those in proximate danger of death receive communion as viaticum. The normative celebration is within Mass, but particular circumstances may prevent a full eucharistic celebration. In either case, the celebration should as far as possible be a communal one involving the participation of the family and loved ones with appropriate readings (Part III), prayers, and even song.

Some of the distinctive features of the revised rite for viaticum are the renewal of the baptismal profession of faith after the homily, the exchange of the sign of peace, the eucharist administered with special words proper to viaticum, and communion under both kinds. Special texts are also provided for the general intercessions and final solemn blessing.

The renewal of baptismal promises takes place after the homily; the dying Christian at the end of life uses the words of the original commitment that has been renewed each Easter and at other important occasions in the course of Christian life. The link between baptism and eucharist at the end of a Christian's earthly sojourn is indeed very close: it is a renewal and fulfillment of initiation into the Christian mysteries, baptism leading to eucharist.

The rites for viaticum may include a sign of peace, whereby the minister and those present embrace the dying Christian. The sign of peace is communicated with a genuine sense of leave-taking, but not without the joy of Christian hope.

The special words accompanying the reception of viaticum underscore that, for the dying Christian, the eucharist is a pledge of resurrection and nourishment for the passage through death: "May the Lord Jesus Christ protect you and lead you to eternal life."

Whenever possible, the Christian departing this earthly life should be communicated under both kinds. This means that wine already consecrated may need to be conveyed in a vessel properly covered so as to eliminate all danger of spilling. At times, reception under the form of wine may also be the only way a dying Christian can receive.

The resolve of the Church to restore viaticum to its proper place as the sacrament intended for the dying is further exemplified by the fact that viaticum now has a ritual format all its own:

Viaticum within Mass	*Viaticum outside Mass*
Introductory Rites	Introductory Rites
	Greeting
	Sprinkling with Holy Water
	Instruction
	Penitential Rite (Apostolic Pardon)
Liturgy of the Word	Liturgy of the Word
Homily	Reading
Baptismal Profession of Faith	Homily
Litany	Baptismal Profession of Faith
	Litany
Liturgy of the Eucharist	Liturgy of Viaticum
Sign of Peace	Lord's Prayer
Communion as Viaticum	Communion as Viaticum
	Silent Prayer
	Prayer after Communion
Concluding Rites	Concluding Rites
Blessing	Blessing
(Apostolic Pardon)	Sign of Peace
Dismissal	

The revised rites for viaticum admittedly present a bit of a problem for the pastoral ministry of the Church. The Church has reinstated viaticum as a sacrament for the dying and reiterated its importance, first articulated at the Council of Nicaea, and has even created a new rite for its celebration. Yet, it is no secret that the sacrament is often neglected. In addition to sudden death, where no recourse to viaticum is possible, the circumstances under which many die, fed intravenously and unable to ingest any other nourishment, also rule out the consumption of the eucharist. The solution to this problem is found by interpreting the distinctive features of its celebration: a communal celebration, ideally the Mass, involving the participation of the sick Christian and others; the renewal of baptismal promises; the sign of peace; communion under two kinds. Although viaticum is a sacrament of passage from this life, the recipient is consistently referred to as being sick, not necessarily in the agony of dying. All this assumes a somewhat earlier time for the ministration of viaticum than was envisioned in the past, just as anointing has been moved up to the beginning of a serious illness. Perhaps the stages of dying discerned by Kübler-Ross might suggest the final stage of acceptance as the proper time to gather the family and friends around the bed of the dying Christian. Viaticum could be a way to ritualize this stage by expressing the Church's resurrection faith in a very forceful and kerygmatic way. The introductory notes wisely specify that should the dying Christian afterward continue to hold on to life, "he or she should be given the opportunity to receive the eucharist as viaticum on successive days, frequently if not daily" (no. 183).

This is an opportunity to say a word about the plenary indulgence, one of the neglected aspects of the revision and the subject of frequent questions posed by priests concerned about the sacramental ministry to the sick and the dying. Whereas the previous Roman Ritual devoted an entire chapter to this apostolic pardon for the hour of death, it goes unmentioned in the introduction to the revised rites and is preserved in only two terse prayers accompanying viaticum and Rites for Exceptional Circumstances. The unhappy and often misunderstood history of indulgences may be a factor in this reticence.

The background to this blessing goes back to the custom of the popes ever since the fourteenth century to confer a plenary indulgence *in articulo mortis*. [26] A precedent for this is found in the solemn absolution preceding viaticum in the thirteenth-century Pontifical of the Roman Curia. The Santorius ritual, one of the sources for the *Rituale Romanum* of 1614, continued this practice but without any official formulary. In 1726, Benedict XIII prescribed a specific text, but only under Benedict XIV was the apostolic blessing entered into the Roman Ritual. In his instruction *Pia Mater* of April 5, 1747, the Pope decreed that henceforth this indulgenced blessing was no longer to be a concession accorded to a privileged few, but was to be delegated to every priest who assisted the dying.

The one form included in the new ritual simply states that the plenary indulgence and pardon of sins comes from the power of the Apostolic See: the language closely resembles the absolution in the *Rite of Penance*. The other prayer gives a more theological reason: this freedom from sin and its aftereffects both now and in the life to come is grounded in the passion and resurrection of Christ. What is the meaning of the Apostolic Pardon? Here is one manner of explanation. If original sin implies a sharing in the sinful condition of the human race and the collective misuse of our freedom, indulgences are a correlative sharing in the good works of the communion of saints. Original sin infers a solidarity in evil; indulgences infer a solidarity in grace with the crucified and risen Lord. From its proper place in the unfolding of rites, the plenary indulgence might be viewed as a prolongation of sacramental penance. Christians have the opportunity to be presented before the Lord in their full integrity of baptismal grace. Thus, the real preparation for the beatific vision is not the sacrament of anointing, as the scholastics once regarded extreme unction, but the Apostolic Pardon, which prepares a dying Christian to see God face to face.

COMMENDATION OF THE DYING (CHAPTER 6)

The models and precedents for the commendation are found in the pages of the New Testament. As he died hanging on the cross, Jesus with the words of Psalm 31:5 on his lips cried out: "Father, into your hands I commit my spirit" (Lk 23:46). The death of the protomartyr Stephen is depicted in similar terms with a plea to forgive his enemies, only this time he prays directly to Christ: "Lord Jesus, receive my spirit" (Acts 7:59).

The earliest liturgical sources for the commendation are the Roman *ordines* dating from the eighth century, which include the commendation as part of a continuous ritual accompanying the Christian from his or her dying moments to as far as the grave.[27] This arrangement reflects a realistic approach to dying and death as part of life, an outlook far removed from ours today. It represents a classic instance of a rite of passage—for the deceased a journey to the Lord; for the mourners moments of separation, transition, and reaggregation. The preparation for death included communion as viaticum, the reading of the passion, and the penitential prayers. Death itself was accompanied by a series of antiphons grouped around the *Subvenite* and Psalm 114 (*In exitu*), as well as a prayer from the Sacramentary.

The commendation of the soul originally referred not to the dying but to the dead: the oration asked God to accept the one who had just died. In the Roman-Frankish liturgical books of the ninth-century Carolingian era, the *commendatio animae* came to mean the group of prayers before death itself. Further developments in the Romano-German Pontifical of the tenth century, as well as in the Pontifical of the Roman Curia of the thirteenth century, led to the arrangement of materials found in the *Rituale Romanum* of 1614.

Before the recent revision, the Roman Ritual included four chapters that pertained to assisting the dying Christian to depart this life: the manner of assisting the dying, the Apostolic Pardon, the order of commendation, and the ministration at the time of death.

In *Pastoral Care*, the revised rites of commendation speak more holistically of commendation of the dying rather than commendation of the soul. The following is the structure of the rite:

Short Texts
Reading
Litany of the Saints
Prayer of Commendation
Prayer after Death
Prayer for the Family and Friends

The short texts from scripture are to be recited with the dying person and may be repeated in a soft, confident tone of voice. Some examples are these:

"Who can separate us from the love of Christ?" (Rom 8:35).
"Whether we live or die, we are the Lord's" (Rom 14:8).
"We have an everlasting home in heaven" (2 Cor 5:1).

This can be both effective and affective when used by those pastorally sensitive to the faith needs of the dying.

The readings include the following:

Job 19:23–27 a: "Job's act of faith is a model for our own; God is the god of the living."
Psalm 23
Psalm 25
Psalm 91
Psalm 121

1 Jn 4:16

Rv 21:1–5 a, 6–7: "God our Father is the God of newness and life; it is his desire that we should come to share his life with him."

Mt 25:1–13: "Jesus bids us be prepared for our ultimate destiny, which is eternal life."

Lk 22:39–46: "Jesus is alive to our pain and sorrow because faithfulness to his Father's will cost him life itself."

Lk 23:44–49: "Jesus' death is witnessed by his friends."

Lk 24:1–8: "Jesus is alive; he gives us eternal life with the Father."

Jn 6:37–40: "Jesus will raise his own from death and give them eternal life."

Jn 14:1–6, 23, 27: "The love of Jesus can raise us up from the sorrow of death to the joy of eternal life."

Other readings from Part III or from the passion of the Lord may also be chosen.

The litany is now reprinted both in its full form and in an abbreviated fashion similar to that found in the *Rite of Baptism for Children*. Special invocations may be inserted so as to mention the patron saints of the dying Christian, the family, and the parish; other devotional forms may also be used.

The prayer of commendation consists of a selection of the best of the medieval treasury of commendation prayers:

"Go forth, Christian soul" (*Profiscere*, no. 220A): This prayer, taken from the eighth-century Gelasian sacramentaries, invokes the names of the Blessed Trinity. At one time it called upon all the archangels and angels and various categories of saints beginning with the patriarchs and prophets: all of whom form a cortege on this supreme journey.

"I commend you" (*Commendo te*, no. 220 B), which although simplified, still includes an extract of a letter of St. Peter Damian (+ 1072).

"Welcome your servant, Lord" (*Suscipe*, no. 220 C), with its present twelve invocations mentions ten personages or groups—at one time there were as many as eighteen—finds a prototype in the eighth-century sacramentaries. Their origin appears to be biblical images used in the old Gelasian sacramentaries for the exorcism of catechumens. Once again, death for a Christian is the perfection of baptism.

"Lord Jesus Christ, Savior of the world" (*Commendamus tibi*, no. 220 D) contains in part a prayer used at Arles already in the sixth century.

"Hail Holy Queen" (*Salve regina*, no. 220 E) is the only devotional prayer as such that has been retained from the earlier assortment of texts.

The prayers after death include the commendation prayer proper to be said after the moment of death as all kneel down. "Saints of God" (*subvenite*) belongs to the oldest stratum of the Roman liturgy for the dead. Other material has been added to fill the pastoral need for recourse to God through prayer at this time. The prayer texts, including Psalm 130 and 23, are for the most part drawn from the *Rite of Funerals*. This procedure, as we have seen, is in keeping with the tradition of the earlier Roman *Ordines* that accompanied the Christian from his or her dying moments to the graveside.

The Prayer for the Family and Friends contains two selections, both borrowed once again from the *Rite of Funerals*: "For the family and friends," and "For the deceased person and for the family and friends." The concluding rubric realizes the importance of the sense of touch:

"For the solace of those present the minister may conclude these prayers with a symbolic gesture, for example, sprinkling the body with holy water, signing the forehead with the sign of the cross, or a simple blessing" (no. 222).

Inasmuch as the commendation of the dying, along with the celebration of viaticum, is one of the least understood and most neglected aspects of the Church's sacramental ministry, a deeper theological appreciation of the commendation rite is in order. Contemporary theology has underscored the importance of the moment of death as a summing up of one's life. Karl Rahner speaks of death as an event involving the whole person, not merely the separation of the soul from the body. Moreover, death is an active rather than a passive recapitulation of one's life.[28] Ladislaus Boros writes of a fundamental option or choice regarding God and the direction of one's life that is reaffirmed in the very moment of death.[29] These optimistic theologies of death as self-transcendence, however, should not overlook some of the darker and more negative features of the act of dying.[30]

The Roman *Ordines* examined above conceived of death as a paschal transition ritual. Viaticum is a pledge of the resurrection; the passion is read until the soul leaves the body in its journey toward God. The psalms used at the beginning (Ps 114) and the end (Ps 116) are Hallel psalms associated with a Jewish paschal meal.[31] The praying Church is present accompanying the dying Christian on this journey. The classic Roman pattern of funerals included processions from the home to the church and from the church to the cemetery. Various prayers, such as the *Subvenite* and the *Chorus angelorum*, reinforced this exodus character of Christian death. In the words of Philippe Rouillard:

"The dying Christian therefore passes from one community to another, and his 'transition' is related to

Christ's passion, either directly (the reading of the Passion) or more often indirectly by referring to the exodus and liberation of Israel. The death of each human being is transfigured by its relation to the Passover of Christ, and is inserted into the great migration of all the people of God on the way towards the kingdom of heaven."[32]

The introductory notes to chapter 6 of *Pastoral Care* support this traditional understanding: the Church seeks to sustain the dying person's union with Christ until this union is brought to fulfillment in death. For this reason the love of the Lord impels Christians to assist their departing brothers and sisters in whatever way possible. (It would be interesting to know why "assisting the dying" has never been explicitly enumerated as a corporal or spiritual work of mercy!) Priests and deacons should make every effort to be present to facilitate this meaning of death in the communion of the Church. In their absence, other members of the community should be prepared to pray the commendation rite. Before all else, the texts— prayers, litanies, aspirations, psalms, and readings— should be adapted to the physical and spiritual condition of the person. They should be said in a slow, quiet voice, alternating with periods of silence. The texts are intended to help the dying person "to face the natural anxiety about death by imitating Christ in his patient suffering and death" (no. 215). Even if the patient is unconscious, the paschal features of the commendation may console the family keeping vigil.

In addition to these ideas from the rite itself, some further pastoral suggestions could be developed along the lines of responsive listening. Never hide behind the mask of the ritual book; as all ritual books do, it serves primarily as a participation aid for the ministers leading the prayer. Try to create an environment in which the person can feel free to talk, to move out of inner isolation to self-expression, particularly if there is some "unfinished business" before the moment of death. It may be necessary to reassure the dying Christian that it is all right to let go and die. Do not be afraid of silence or tears and other signs of emotion and caring. Always show a profound respect: we cannot assume to know everything that is going on inside the patient or to have all the answers. We are fellow travelers, companions sharing the same mortal destiny in our pilgrimage to God. More important than what we say or do is a sense of personal presence as believing human beings who understand, love, and allow the patient's pain to touch us. Do not be afraid of the sense of touch. It speaks a language far louder than words. Hearing and touch are the last senses to fail us. The commendation rite wisely directs the baptismal sign of the cross to be made on the forehead of the dying Christian; one would have also liked to read something about the even more elementary gesture of holding the person's hand.

Deathbed scenes of saints and worthies of the past are usually pictured in a room crowded with family and friends. Today people often die alone, one of the greatest fears that afflict the elderly. If the Church has restored viaticum as a sacrament for the dying with a canonical insistence on its ministration and a ritual format all its own, perhaps a similar priority should be assigned to the use of the rite of Commendation of the Dying whenever possible.

PRAYERS FOR THE DEAD (CHAPTER 7)

It is one thing for a priest to inform a grieving family that he is unable to anoint their loved one because he or she is already dead. It is another to suggest to the minister what course of action to take in this highly charged emotional atmosphere. This pastoral need has now been remedied by the newly created prayers designed to comfort the distraught family and friends on those occasions when the sacrament of anointing cannot be celebrated. As important as the rite itself is the introductory note of explanation for the family of the deceased "that sacraments are celebrated for the living, not for the dead, and that the dead are effectively helped by the prayers of the living." The underlying problem here is the critical need for better catechesis on the meaning of the sacrament of anointing in parish life.

The outline of the rite is as follows:

Greeting
Prayer
Reading
Litany
Lord's Prayer
Prayer of Commendation

Two options are provided for the greeting, one taken from the funeral ritual, the other a new composition:

"In this moment of sorrow
the Lord is in our midst
and comforts us with his word:
Blessed are the sorrowful; they shall be consoled" (no. 226).

These greetings are suggestions only, and a spontaneous greeting may be another appropriate way to begin.

The two prayer options are both from the *Rite of Funerals*. The readings may be taken from Part III, two of which are reprinted: Luke 23:44–46 (death of Jesus) and John 11 (raising of Lazarus). Once again, the symbolic gesture of sprinkling the body with holy water, signing the forehead with the sign of the cross, or a simple blessing is suggested in the final rubric. This difficult situation is not the time for a lengthy exposition on the mystery of suffering and evil, but rather a time for the minister of the Church to be present and available to people in need.

RITES FOR EXCEPTIONAL CIRCUMSTANCES (CHAPTER 8)
The phrase "exceptional circumstances" is chosen deliberately; these rites are only to be used in case of a genuine necessity when an immediate danger of death makes impossible a more developed form of pastoral care.

Continuous Rite of Penance, Anointing, and Viaticum
The Continuous Rite provides for the celebration of these sacraments within a single service. When requested, the sacrament of penance is to be adapted to the dying person's condition and should take place before the anointing and the reception of viaticum.

When death is imminent, a single anointing followed by viaticum suffice. Where the situation is extreme, viaticum should be given immediately with or without anointing. This is one more indication of the high priority the Church assigns to viaticum as a sacrament for the dying.

Because of the concentration of sacraments and confusion concerning two different uses of oil, the rite goes on to suggest that the sacrament of anointing (oil of the sick) and the sacrament of confirmation (chrism) not be performed in a continuous rite. If the dying person needs to be confirmed, the sacrament would be celebrated before the blessing of the oil of the sick; in this case, the laying on of hands as part of the anointing liturgy would be omitted. Under extreme circumstances such as these, it would seem that the full sacramental initiation as a Christian takes precedence over the sacrament of anointing.

The outline of the rite will be of assistance in following the improved format of a service in which as many as four sacraments might be celebrated:

Introductory Rites
  Greeting
  Instruction
Liturgy of Penance
  Sacrament of Penance
  (Penitential Rite)
  (Apostolic Pardon)
  Baptismal Profession of Faith
  Litany
(Liturgy of Confirmation)
Liturgy of Anointing
  Laying on of Hands
  Prayer over the Oil
  Anointing
  (Prayer after Anointing)
Liturgy of Viaticum
  Lord's Prayer
  Communion as Viaticum
  Silent Prayer
  Prayer after Communion
Concluding Rites
  Blessing
  Sign of Peace
  (Prayer after Death)

As is readily apparent, the Apostolic Pardon properly serves as an extension of the sacramental penance. The original sequence of anointing to be followed by viaticum has also been recovered.

One might, however, seriously question the propriety of this overall arrangement of rites. When death is imminent, why is the anointing of the sick required at all? Why not just reconciliation and viaticum? If anointing is clearly restored as a sacrament for the seriously ill, in those situations where impending

death is the paramount consideration, why this
insistence on anointing of the sick?

Rite for Emergencies
"Emergencies" are understood to be extreme
circumstances when even the Continuous Rite cannot
be celebrated, be this a sudden danger of death from
injury or illness, or instances where the priest is
summoned when the person is at the point of death. In
order to forestall a rushed and impersonal ministration,
even here the priest is to offer "every possible ministry
of the Church as reverently and expeditiously as he
can" (no. 260). He may also appropriate other prayers
from the ritual to help the dying person and the others
present.

The order of service would be the sacrament of
penance, at the wish of the dying Christian,
communion as viaticum, and finally, if there is still
time, the sacrament of anointing.

Sacrament of Penance
(Apostolic Pardon)
Lord's Prayer
Communion as Viaticum
(Prayer before Anointing)
Anointing
Concluding Prayer
Blessing
Sign of Peace

After this abbreviated rite for emergencies, the priest
could continue in prayer with the dying person,
family, and friends with selections taken from the
Commendation of the Dying.

Once again, if the person has already died, the priest is
not to anoint but is to console the family with prayers
found at the conclusion of the commendation rite.
Only where there is reason to believe the person is still

living, the priest may anoint conditionally, introducing the sacramental form with the words: "If life is in you . . . ."

A similar critique as before arises regarding the propriety of anointing a dying Christian when reconciliation and viaticum are the more obvious sacramental needs. What is more, the anointing of a moribund person even *after* viaticum suggests once again the "extreme unction" perception of the sacrament.

Christian Initiation for the Dying
The 1973 provisional ritual contained a chapter on Confirmation of a Person in Danger of Death. Three possible occasions come to mind for which this would be necessary: a baptized infant, a child of catechetical age, and an adult who was never confirmed. Perhaps as a result of the impact of the Church's revision of its initiation sacraments, *Pastoral Care* provides a more complete format that includes whatever initiation sacraments may be wanting.

Introductory Rites
   Greeting
   Dialogue
Liturgy of the Word
   Gospel Reading
   Litany
Liturgy of Christian Initiation
   Renunciation of Sin
   Profession of Faith
   Baptism
   (Anointing after Baptism)
   Confirmation
   Lord's Prayer
   Communion as Viaticum
   Prayer after Communion

Concluding Rites
    Blessing
    Sign of Peace

Normally, the *Rite of Christian Initiation of Adults* should
be celebrated in it fullness over a period of time. When
this is not possible, the short rite may be used. The
various ministers are specified: when there is not a
priest or deacon, any member of the faithful may
baptize; a priest may confirm a person in danger of
death; viaticum may be celebrated by a priest, deacon,
or eucharistic minister. Pared down to the bone,
baptism would consist of the pouring of water (blessed
or natural) with the appropriate words. Catechumens
and those baptized in proximate danger of death who
later recover their health are expected to complete their
Christian formation afterwards.

The introductory notes for the care of a dying child also
provide for the fullness of sacramental initiation,
seemingly encouraging the reception of the eucharist,
if need be, even by infants. All this makes abundant
good sense, for every reason used to support infant
baptism can also be used to substantiate infant
communion.

CONCLUSION
We have explored the reformed rites for the dying. An
analysis of the Church's prayer for the dying has
yielded a rich harvest of images of death as sleep and
eternal repose, as birth into light, refreshment, and
peace, as a journey to the Lord. The tradition of
viaticum, the eucharist received as "food for the
journey," makes all the more imperative the recovery
in pastoral praxis of this much-neglected sacrament for
the dying. As has been pointed out, Part II of *Pastoral
Care of the Sick: Rites of Anointing and Viaticum* is as
much concerned with the ministry to the dying as Part

I of the same ritual is with the ministry to the sick. Lest the ministry to the dying be perceived as just one further way of coping with the unpleasantness of death, albeit under a religious guise, the powerful words of Alexander Schmemann call us to rediscover a proper set of priorities. The Christian revelation of Christ as Life reveals the theological truth about death:

"Christianity is not reconciliation with death. It is the revelation of death, and it reveals death because it is the revelation of Life. Christ is this Life. And only if Christ is Life is death what Christianity proclaims it to be, namely the enemy to be destroyed and not a 'mystery' to be explained. Religion and secularism, by explaining death, give it a 'status,' a rationale, make it 'normal.' Only Christianity proclaims it to be *abnormal* and, therefore, truly horrible. At the grave of Lazarus Christ wept, and when His own hour to die approached, 'he began to be sore amazed and very heavy.' In the light of Christ, *this* world, this *life* are lost and are beyond mere 'help,' not because there is fear of death in them, but because they have accepted and normalized death. To accept God's world as a cosmic cemetery which is to be abolished and replaced by an 'other world' which looks like a cemetery (eternal rest) and to call this religion, to live in a cosmic cemetery and to 'dispose' every day of thousands of corpses and to get excited about a 'just society' and to be happy!—this is the fall of man. It is not the immorality or the crimes of man that reveal him as a fallen being; it is his 'positive ideal'—religious or secular—and his satisfaction with this ideal. This fall, however, can be truly revealed only by Christ, because only in Christ is the *fullness of life* revealed to us, and death, therefore, becomes 'awful,' the very fall from life, the enemy. It is *this world* (and not any 'other world'), it is *this life* (and not some 'other life') that were given to man to be a sacrament of the divine presence, given as communion with God, and it is only through this world, this life, by 'transforming' them into communion with God that man *was to be*. The horror of death is, therefore, not in its being the 'end' and not in physical destruction. By being separation from the world and life, it is *separation from God*. The dead cannot glorify God. It is, in other words, when Christ reveals Life to us that we can hear the Christian message about death as the enemy of God. It is when Life weeps at the grave of the friend, when it contemplates the horror of death, that the victory over death begins."[33]

NOTES

1.   I am grateful to Rev. Robert Reeves for these pastoral reflections on the psychology of dying.

2.   Julia Upton, "A Place to Die," *Liturgy* 25 (1980) 18–21; Michael Hamilton and Helen Reid (eds.), *A Hospice Handbook* (Grand Rapids, Mich.: Eerdmans, 1980).

3.   Elisabeth Kübler-Ross, *On Death and Dying* (New York: Macmillan, 1969); *Questions and Answers on Death and Dying* (New York: Macmillan, 1974); *Death, the Final Stage of Growth* (Englewood Cliffs, N.J.: Prentice-Hall, 1975); *Living with Death and Dying* (New York: Macmillan, 1981); *To Live until We Say Goodbye*. Photos by Mal Warshaw (Englewood Cliffs: Prentice-Hall, 1978).

4.   Peter Berger, *A Rumor of Angels* (New York: Doubleday, 1969) 72–81.

5.   Alfred C. Rush, *Death and Burial in Christian Antiquity* (Washington, D.C.: 1941) 1–87; Fr. Louvel, "Les themes bibliques de las liturgie des defunts," La Maison-Dieu 44 (1955) 29–48; B. Botte, "The Earliest Formulas of Prayer for the Dead," in *Temple of the Holy Spirit: Sickness and Death of the Christian in the Liturgy* (New York: Pueblo, 1983) 17–32; Richard Rutherford, *The Death of a Christian: The Rite of Funerals* (New York: Pueblo, 1980).

6.   *Rite of Funerals*, para. 47.

7. Raymond Moody, *Life After Life* (Atlanta: Mockingbird Books, 1975).

8. *Rite of Funerals*, para. 50.

9. See also Damien Sicard, "Preparation for Death and Prayer for the Dying," in *Temple of the Holy Spirit* 239–46.

10. Ignatius, *Ad Romanos* 6, as cited in Alfred Rush, "The Eucharist, the Sacrament of the Dying in Christian Antiquity," *The Jurist* 34 (1974) 13–14. See *Early Christian Writings. The Apostolic Fathers*, trans. Maxwell Staniforth (London: Penguin, 1968) 105–6.

11. *Ad Romanos* 7; *The Apostolic Fathers*, p. 106.

12. *Ad Ephesios* 20; *The Apostolic Fathers*, p. 82.

13. "The Martyrdom of Polycarp" 14; *The Apostolic Fathers*, pp. 160–161.

14. Lambert Beauduin, "Le viatique," *La Maison-Dieu* 15 (1948) 117–129; Gregory Grabka, "Christian Viaticum: A Study of Its Cultural Background," *Traditio* 9 (1953) 1–43; Otto Nussbaum, *Die Aufbewahrung der Eucharistie* (Bonn: Hanstein, 1979) 62–101; Damien Sicard, "Le viatique: perspectives nouvelles?" *La Maison-Dieu* 113 (1973) 103–14.

15. Eusebius, *Historia ecclesiastica* 6, 44, 2–6 (Griechische Christliche Schriftsteller der Ersten drei Jahrhunderts 2. 624f).

16. Denzinger-Schönmetzer no. 129.

17. Paulinus, *Vita S. Ambrosii* 47 (PL 14. 43).

18. Palladius, *De vita et conversatione Beati Joannis Chrysostomi* 11 (PG 47.38).

19. Vita S. Melaniae 68. Mariano Card. Rampolla, *Santa Melania* (Rome, 1905) 39.

20. *Dialogi* 2. 37 (PL 66. 202).

21. Grabka, "Christian Viaticum" 37–38.

22. An edition of this ordo is found in Damien Sicard, *La liturgie de la mort dans l'église latine des origines a la réforme carolingienne*, Liturgiegeschichtliche Quellen und Forschungen, no. 63 (Munster: Aschendorff, 1978) 8.

23. Michel Andrieu, Les "Ordines Romani" du haut moyen age IV (Louvain: Spicilegium, 1956) 529–30. See also C. Vogel and R. Elze, Le Pontifical Romano-Germanique du dixième siècle. Studie testi 226–27, (Vatican, 1963).

24. P.M. Gy, "La mort du chrétien," in L'église en prière, ed. A.G. Martimort (Paris: Descleé, 3rd rev. ed. 1965) 636–40, surveys this development in which the Roman Rite for viaticum is substantially complete by the thirteenth century.

25. A. Franz, Das Rituale von St. Florian aus dem zwölften Jahrhundert (Freiburg: Herder, 1904) 82. See also A.G. Martimort, "L'ordo commendationis animae," La Maison-Dieu 15 (1948) 143–60.

26. A. G . Martimort, "Pastorale liturgique des malades," Questions liturgiques et pastorales 36 (1965) 231–43.

27. Sicard, La liturgie de la mort, 1–33, Andrieu, Les "Ordines Romani" 529. See also A.G. Martimort, "Comment meurt un chrétien," La Maison-Dieu 44 (1955) 5–28.

28. Karl Rahner, On the Theology of Death, Quaestiones Disputatae 2 (New York: Herder, 1961).

29. Ladislaus Boros, The Mystery of Death (New York: Herder, 1965).

30. Bartholomew Collopy, "Theology and Death," Theological Studies 39 (March 1978) 22–54.

31. Nahum Glatzer (ed.), The Passover Haggadah (New York: Schocken Books, 1969).

32. Philippe Rouillard, "The Liturgy of the Dead as a Rite of Passage," Liturgy and Human Passage (Concilium) ed. David Power and Luis Maldonado (New York: Seabury, 1979) 77–78.

33. Alexander Schmemann, For the Life of the World (New York: St. Vladimir Seminary Press, 1973) 99–100.

Present and Future

Chapter Four

Theological Dimensions
of Sickness and Healing

A theology of sickness and healing is one of the most
contemporary and controversial topics among
Christians. It is contemporary because of the current
concern in the churches for healing, especially among
pentecostal-charismatic groups, and also because of the
interest generated by the revised Roman Catholic *Rite
of Anointing and Pastoral Care of the Sick* (December 7,
1972). The theme of sickness and healing is
controversial because of the many attendant and
theologically complex issues, such as Christian
anthropology, the mystery of suffering and evil
(theodicy), the meaning of the healing activity of Jesus
(biblical exegesis), the role of suffering in the life of
Christ and his disciples (Christology), the abiding place
of healing in the mission of the Christian Church
(ecclesiology), and the relationship between
charismatic and sacramental healing. While no
exhaustive claim can be made toward providing all the
answers, at least the questions should be posed
adequately.

THE TOTAL HUMAN PERSON
What does it mean to be seriously ill? Sickness
represents a crisis situation in the life of the person
who is ill.[1] First of all, there is a crisis of
communication with oneself: the human body is no
longer experienced as an extension of one's inner
being, but has become an instrument to be exposed,

139

probed, poked, and manipulated by all who would provide for its care. Besides this spatial disability there is also a temporal one, for life is lived in the boredom of a disconnected present that has lost all orientation to past and future. "When will I come home from the hospital? When will I get better?"

Similar to Kübler-Ross' stages of dying are the stages discernible in a serious illness. There is an initial period of silence: the ill do not wish to talk and are given to superficial exchanges, so emotionally taken up are they with sickness. In the next period of aggression, one lashes out at one's milieu: the seemingly infrequent visits of family and friends, the perceived incompetence of the medical staff and hospital personnel, the apparent neglect of the Church. At this point, it is important for friends, family, and pastoral ministers not to take this reaction as a personal affront, but rather as an impassioned cry for help, for love and understanding, for a simple personal presence. A period of depression and rebirth follows. This is a fruitful time for interiorization, when one begins to take stock of the situation and of oneself. Finally, there is a period of acceptance or negation in which the affliction is either endured with serenity or met with contempt and revolt ("I can, I will, get better.") The famous prayer used by Alcoholics Anonymous captures this reaction: "Lord, give me courage to change the things that can be changed, serenity to accept what cannot be changed, and wisdom to know the difference."

Sickness is also a crisis of communication with others within one's total environment. The experience of life as it is normally lived is disrupted. Especially when confined to a hospital, one is isolated from the usual activities: the family, work or profession, circle of friends, those things and relationships that make life most worth living. J.H. van den Berg describes the existential plight of a husband and father who discovers himself ill upon awakening—actually a sickness of no great consequence—and who decides to stay in bed:

"Then, slowly, but irrevocably, a change, characteristic of the sickbed, establishes itself. I hear the day begin. From downstairs the sounds of household activities penetrate into the bedroom. The children are called for breakfast. Loud hasty voices are evidence of the fact that their owners have to go to school in a few minutes. A handkerchief has to be found, and a bookbag. Quick young legs run up and down the stairs. How familiar, and at the same time how utterly strange things are; how near and yet how far away they are. What I am hearing is the beginning of my daily existence, with this difference, though, that now I have no function in it. In a way I still belong completely to what happens downstairs; I take a share in the noises I hear, but at the same time everything passes me by, everything happens at a great distance. 'Is Daddy ill?' a voice calls out; even at this early moment, it has ceased to consider that I can hear it. 'Yes, Daddy is ill.' A moment later the door opens and they come to say goodbye. They remain just as remote. The distance I measured in the sounds from downstairs appears even greater, if possible, now that they are at my bedside, with their fresh clean faces and lively gestures. Everything about them indicates the normal healthy day, the day of work and play, of street and school. The day outside the house, in which 'outside' has acquired a new special meaning for me, a meaning emphasizing my exclusion."[2]

There is further a crisis of communication with the Church often experienced by Christians who have been active in their parishes and now feel forgotten and forsaken. Before any institutionalized rite, the Church through its ministers and faithful should demonstrate a personal presence, not just the administration of another sacrament or an attempt to hide behind a ritual mask. Above all, the Church should strive to be a prophetic sign, a counterculture amid a contemporary society that idolizes youth, beauty, and health. In this way, the Church can enable the sick and dying to put aside the cruel and lonely game of playacting and become their freest and truest selves. Perhaps the most important statement the Second Vatican Council made about anointing and the pastoral care of the sick is not found in the *Constitution on the Sacred Liturgy* but rather in paragraph 11 of the *Constitution on the Church:*

"By the sacred anointing of the sick and the prayer of the priests the whole Church commends those who are ill to the suffering and glorified Lord that he may raise them up and save them (cf. Jas 5:14–16). And indeed she exhorts them to contribute to the good of the people of God by freely uniting themselves to the passion and death of Christ (cf. Rom 8:17; Col 1:24; 2 Tm 2:11–12; 1 Pt 4:13)."[3]

Last but certainly not least, sickness constitutes a crisis situation in one's relationship with God. Sickness causes one to ask questions not normally raised regarding the meaning of life, death, and faith. There is a confrontation with human finitude and the eventuality of death: "I will disappear physically, affectively, socially." God often seems distant and unloving. There is the almost universal phenomenon of guilt: "What did I do wrong? Why is God punishing me?" Serious illness thus presents a temptation to one's faith in God. It is an ambivalent situation for either growth and holiness or else regression and possible despair. The revised rites for the sick intuitively grasp this liminal predicament:

"Those who are seriously ill need the special help of God's grace in this time of anxiety, lest they be broken in spirit and, under the pressure of temptation, perhaps weakened in their faith" (no. 5).

In a word, when one is seriously ill, the condition has implications that affect one's entire well-being.

What is needed is not a kind of unconscious dualism, but a holistic Christian anthropology of the human person as psychosomatic unity. A consistent biblical anthropology antedating the advent of Hellenistic and later Cartesian dualism perceives the human person as an animated body. For example, the book of Psalms— the prayer book of the Bible—could provide some guidance in those psalms such as Psalm 6, which vividly depicts the existential plight of the sick:

"Be gracious to me, O Lord, for I am languishing;
O Lord, heal me, for my bones are troubled.
My soul also is sorely troubled.
But thou, O Lord—how long?"

Or again, Psalm 22:

"I am poured out like water,
   and all my bones are out of joint;
my heart is like wax,
   it is melted within my breast;
my strength is dried up like a potsherd,
and my tongue cleaves to my jaws;
thou dost lay me in the dust of death."[4]

Contemporary theology also moves in this direction: the human person is a spirit in the world, an incarnate spirit. In the theology of Karl Rahner, this bodily orientation continues even after death through a new relationship to the created universe.[5]

Some insight might also be gained from an examination of human wholeness from the perspective of C.G. Jung's depth psychology.[6] Perhaps this could shed some light on the ancient phenomenon of "incubation," a kind of "sleeping-in" state whereby the sick and ailing would make a pilgrimage to a shrine or temple, induce pleasant thoughts of recovery through association with the deity or saint, sleep in the precincts of the building, and awaken cured.[7] Or again, more exploration is needed into the psychogenesis of sickness, including certain types of cancer especially prevalent among people living under stress-filled conditions.

Jung's "individuation" is a psychic process of development leading toward wholeness, although never complete in this life. Individuation consists of a synthesis of the conscious and unconscious personalities. If the unconscious can be a source of illness, it can also be a source of healing that results when the contents of the unconscious are made conscious. Psychologist Victor Frankl concurs with Jung's contention that most people's psychological difficulties have spiritual roots and that the most important need is for a sense of meaning and purpose in life, that is, a positive outlook.[8]

Insights from depth psychology have already been applied to the spiritual life and prayer, for example, mantra prayers (the Eastern "Jesus Prayer" and the rosary of the Western Church) and an oval mandala object (use of a monstrance for eucharistic exposition) that distract the conscious mind to tap into the rich affectivity of the unconscious. Application should also be made to charismatic healing techniques such as the "healing of the memories" to discern how both nature and grace work together, without resorting immediately to a notion of the miraculous.[9] Something of depth psychology may also lie behind the new emphases in holistic medicine that through diet, simple care, and positive outlook seek to release a natural curative process known as the *vis mediatrix naturae*. [10]

A wise physician once remarked that there is no such thing as sickness in itself, only people who are sick. This comment should serve as a safeguard against the danger of abstraction in theologizing about human illness. Sickness is a very real phenomenon that confronts the total human person.

THE MYSTERY OF SUFFERING AND EVIL

Theodicy is an attempt to resolve the apparent contradiction between God's justice and goodness and the fact of evil. Rather than resorting to mystery when confronted with a logical impasse, it would be more forthright to begin with mystery from the start, for no clear answer is to be found in scripture. The book of Job leaves this mystery of suffering and evil unresolved; the New Testament proclaims the theological paradox of the cross. Sometimes there is no apparent reason why bad things happen to good people. Vulnerability to death is one of the given conditions of human life in the imperfect, developing world we live in. Yet, no matter how bad things become, human beings are still free to make choices about life, challenged to make the best out of difficult situations, to transform pain and suffering into growth experiences. [11]

Two classical approaches have been suggested: an Augustinian theodicy of free will that has been handed down in the Western Church and has found a contemporary exponent in Karl Rahner; and an Irenaean theodicy of development transmitted in the Eastern Church, which finds expression in the thought of Teilhard de Chardin. [12]

The Augustinian theodicy of free will looks upon evil as a privation of good. The original harmony of the cosmos intended by the Creator was upset through the misuse of human freedom from the beginning, what we have come to know as original sin. Evil can be distinguished according to natural or moral evil, suffering distinguished according to that which comes from normal growth and maturation and that which is attributable to sin. A negative criticism of this theodicy of free will is that it is too static and works with an insufficient grasp of history and eschatology. Positively, this approach rightly senses some undefinable relationship between sin and sickness. The manner in which we experience suffering and sickness, the often acute pain and unrelieved anguish, are the result of a sinful disharmony in creation that is "groaning in travail" awaiting its deliverance (Rm 8:22).

The Irenaean theodicy of development, with its roots in the hopeful theology of Ireaneus of Lyons (d. c. 202), would locate the perfect harmony and order of creation not at the beginning but at the end of history. According to this evolutionary world view, evil and suffering are a "vale of soul making," an opportunity for growth and transcendence, although Teilhard de Chardin does admit the possibility of a "primal catastrophe" or Fall. Positively, this approach is more in keeping with the thrust of salvation history, as well as with a theology of hope and contemporary eschatology. [13] A shortcoming could be its excessive optimism about suffering, especially after the Holocaust of European Jewry and the advent of the nuclear age.

Process theology also has some promising insights on theodicy through its more dynamic view of God: to love is to change, to suffer. The history of the suffering in the world is included in the story of God because of the story of Christ's suffering. As Whitehead, the foremost exponent of process theology, put it: "In this sense, God is the great companion—the fellow sufferer who understands."[14] Without adopting the total process package, we could at least begin to take the incarnation more seriously, with the humanity of Jesus as the starting point.

For our purposes here, three summary statements about this inexhaustible mystery are in order:

1. Some relationship exists between sin and sickness. The Greek verb, "to save" (*sōzein*), used most frequently in the healing works of Jesus ("Your faith has saved you"), bears a twofold meaning at times used interchangeably: salvation from sin, and salvation from sickness and disease. A similar meaning is conveyed through the English word "health," which in earlier times denoted spiritual, physical, or mental soundness, even salvation, for example, in Morning Prayer from *The Book of Common Prayer:* "We have left undone those things which we ought to have done, and there is no health in us." Or again, the prescription in James 5:14–15a on anointing the sick is concluded with an admonition: ". . . and if he has committed sins, he will be forgiven. Therefore confess your sins to one another, and pray for one another, that you may be healed" (James 5:15b–16). Perhaps this truth was also at the heart of the medieval scholastic teaching on original sin and the subsequent loss of the preternatural gifts of immortality, integrity, knowledge, and freedom from pain and suffering. In other words, sin—both the sin of the world and our own personal sins—has cosmic ramifications in terms of human solidarity and the ordering of the cosmos. This relationship between sin and sickness should not be misconstrued, however, in a simplistic sense that personal sin caused a given illness, a false view corrected by Jesus himself: "It was not that this man sinned or his parents, but that the works of God might be manifest in him" (John 9:3). Nor is sickness a means

of divine vindication by an irate God who rains down chastisement upon disobedient children, another false avenue that has made the Office of the Visitation of the Sick in the Anglican *Book of Common Prayer* so embarrassing and difficult to use. Rather, the whole human person suffers sickness as a consequence of evil in the world.

2. We should therefore be mindful not to blame God directly for sickness, as if God were its author. God reacts to and respects humanity's use, and lamentable misuse, of its freedom. This is a misunderstanding still deeply imbedded in the hearts of many good people who somehow revert to a "God of the ambush," instead of the New Testament revelation of the God we dare to call "Father." In other words, God is on our side.

3. The promised salvation in Jesus Christ encompasses the total person, for its goal is none other than the resurrection of all flesh (1 Cor 15). In this holistic vision of the human race, Jesus has come to free us, to heal us from sin and evil and all its manifestations, so that we can grow to full stature as children of God.

JESUS' MINISTRY TO THE SICK

Jesus' ministry to the sick is one of healing in the widest sense: "Those who are well have no need of a physician, but those who are sick; I came not to call the righteous, but sinners" (Mk 2:17). Jesus has come as a compassionate doctor to cure an ailing human race cast into a fallen-sin-sickness situation. In its mission to the nations, the Church very early recognized, and quickly rejected, a parallelism between Christ and Asklepius, the god of healing in the ancient world.[15] This broad-based ministry of healing is evident in the account of the woman caught in adultery (Jn 8:1–11). It is a ministry of listening, for Jesus utters not a word until the end; a ministry of affirming ("Neither do I condemn you"); a ministry of freeing ("Go, and do not sin again"). [16] Healing (Healer) is synonymous with Jesus' life and ministry, together with other scriptural images such as reconciliation, salvation (Savior), redemption (Redeemer), justification, recapitulation, and liberation. If human sickness derives from our sinful alienation, therefore, healing is a divine reality that aims primarily at our wholeness before a transcendent God, a restoration or reconciliation that can bring about secondarily a temporal healing.

Healing Works as Eschatological Signs of the Kingdom
We often labor under the notion of miracle inherited from the age of enlightenment, whereby a miracle is perceived as a supernatural act contrary to the laws of nature and hence an apologetic proof of divine intervention. To this must be contrasted the scriptural viewpoint that just as word and action go together in the revelation of God, so also do creation and salvation form a unity. Thus a close affinity exists between nature miracles (for example, calming the sea) and healing miracles. A characteristic of the reign of Satan is Satan's hostility to creation. And lest Jesus be taken simply as a kind of thaumaturgical wonder man, the gospels generally avoid the conventional terms miracle or wonder in preference for the more modest "act of power" (*dynamis*) in the synoptics, "works" (*terata*) and "signs" (*semeia*) in John's gospel. [17]

Yet, the healing activity of Jesus of Nazareth is central to the New Testament. [18] Mark's gospel alone records over twenty individual acts of healing, so that roughly one-half of his gospel is given over to healing narratives. In the Acts of the Apostles, the witness of Jesus' healing activity is likewise integral to Peter's kerygma on Pentecost Sunday (Acts 2:22) and elsewhere. In other words, the key question is not whether the healing works took place (which is assumed) or how they happened (possibly psychological suggestion in some instances) but rather what they mean.

The disciples of John the Baptizer approach Jesus to ask if he is the long-awaited Messiah who is to come (Mt 11:2–5; Lk 7:18–23). Jesus' response, involving the categories of Isaiah 35, contains an imagery that goes beyond physical healing: the "blind" are able to see the glory of God, "cripples" can walk in the paths of God, "lepers" are cleansed of their sins, "deaf" people hear the good news, the "dead" are raised to new life in Christ, and the "poor" become rich through the preaching of the gospel. Similarly, the seven signs of the fourth gospel, three of which are healing miracles, have a deep underlying meaning. For example, the man born blind (Jn 9:1–34) portrays Jesus as the light of the world; the raising of Lazarus (Jn 11:1–44) points to Jesus as the resurrection and the life.

The healing works of Jesus are therefore to be understood as signs of the kingdom proclaimed in the gospel as a new reign of peace and justice in which God will put an end to the ancient enemies of the human race: sin and evil, sickness and death. The healing works of Jesus are eschatological signs in the sense of the "already" and the "not yet." His "acts of power" foreshadow the ultimate transformation of humanity and of the universe on the day of Jesus' Second Coming, the resurrection of all flesh, an event not yet come to pass. The blind man and Lazarus will eventually die, but the healing works on their behalf indicate, however briefly, something of the healing transformation that will take place on the last day. At the same time, the healing miracles are eschatological signs of an "already" dimension of the kingdom, which is at work in the world through the present offer of eternal life and communion with God that begins in this life. This appears to have been the understanding of later Christians, who in the early Church transposed features of Jesus' healing ministry into the rites of Christian initiation: exorcisms, profession of faith, *ephphetha* rite (Mk 7:34), anointing with oil (Mk 6:13), bathing in water (Jn 9), and the laying on of hands. In other words, the Risen Lord personally enters into our lives, touches and heals us now in baptism.[19]

In passing, further similarities between the healing works of Jesus and the Christian sacraments may be observed. First of all, both bring about what they signify: the healing works are signs that announce the kingdom and usher it in; so also the sacraments signify the saving presence of God and also effect what they signify.[20] Second, in both the healing experiences and the sacramental encounters, the response of faith and conversion is essential.[21] Neither is magic or automatic: the beneficiaries — the individual recipients and the witnessing community — are expected to behave as persons whose lives have been radically changed.

The Healing Death and Resurrection: The Paschal Mystery
To all this must be quickly added that human wholeness is always a relative concept in this life. The ultimate healing transformation comes from suffering and death borne out of love. This is how the kingdom of God advances. This is how Jesus became the Risen Christ and how we too personally share in the Easter victory of the Lord. This is what the paschal mystery is about, and scripture could scarcely be more explicit on this point. "If any man would come after me, let him deny himself and take up his cross daily and follow me. For whoever would save his life will lose it; and whoever loses his life for my sake, he will save it" (Lk 9:23, 24).

The Risen Lord confronts and consoles his distraught disciples at Emmaus: "Was it not necessary that the

Christ should suffer these things and enter into his glory" (Lk 24:26). He tells the doubting Thomas: "Put your finger here, and see my hands; and put out your hand, and place it in my side" (Jn 20:27). Even in his glorified humanity the Risen Christ still bears the marks of his crucifixion. His very wounds are healing and life-giving (1 Pt 2:24). "Worthy is the Lamb who was slain, to receive power and wealth and wisdom and might and honor and glory and blessing" (Rv 5:12).

An authentic Pauline mysticism strives for union with the crucified and risen one: a conformation that begins at baptism (Rom 6:3–11) and glories in the cross (Gal 6:14) as the only way toward full communion with the Beloved. And while Paul graphically depicts the sufferings that come from his apostolate, the celebrated "thorn in the flesh" (2 Cor 12:7) would seem not to exclude the misery that comes from ill health. Far from a misguided spirituality that seeks to justify suffering for suffering's sake, and as equally distanced from the opposite extreme that fails to see that the Easter issues forth from the passion of Good Friday, St. Paul captures the dynamic passage of sharing in Jesus' life-giving death and resurrection when he prays "that I may know him and the power of his resurrection, and may share his sufferings, becoming like him in his death, that if possible I may attain the resurrection from the dead" (Phil 3:10, 11). Death is not so much a friend as it is the last hurdle to be overcome before a complete sharing in Christ's paschal triumph: "the last enemy to be destroyed is death" (1 Cor 15:26).

The message of the fourth gospel is similar: "Unless the grain of wheat falls into the earth and dies, it remains alone; but if it dies, it bears much fruit" (Jn 12:24). The driving force behind this ultimate healing through suffering and death is love. As John begins his account of the Last Supper and passion: "Now before the feast of the Passover, when Jesus knew that his hour had come to depart out of this world to the Father, having loved his own who were in the world, he loved them to the end" (Jn 13:1). The cross theology of John's gospel further reveals that Jesus' "lifting up" on the cross—a turn of phrase that refers to the cross as both an instrument of torture and a way to exaltation—is the manner whereby Jesus will draw all people to himself (Jn 12:32). Finally, the blood and water flowing from the pierced side of the Lord are an indication to the author of the fourth gospel that the crucifixion, resurrection, and outpouring of the Spirit are intimately bound together (Jn 19:34).

The paradoxical predicament of Christian existence confronted by illness is captured in the introductory paragraphs to the revised *Pastoral Care of the Sick* (nos. 1–4) on human sickness and its meaning in the mystery of salvation. On the one hand, we are challenged to struggle against sickness and seek the blessing of good health in the name of Jesus. On the other hand, there is a clear realization that ultimate healing is not found in this life but comes rather from loving communion in the Lord's dying and rising. To deny this would be to fall inadvertently into the hands of the very death-denying culture the Church seeks to evangelize:

"Part of the plan laid out by God's providence is that we should fight strenuously against all sickness and carefully seek the blessings of good health, so that we may fulfill our role in human society and in the Church. Yet we should always be prepared to fill up what is lacking in Christ's sufferings for the salvation of the world as we look forward to creation's being set free in the glory of the children of God (see Colossians 1:24; Romans 8:19–21).

"Moreover, the role of the sick in the Church is to be a reminder to others of the essential or higher things. By their witness the sick show that our mortal life must be redeemed through the mystery of Christ's death and resurrection" (no. 3).

Participation in the paschal mystery is especially manifest among those who are sick and dying. Because of the healing death and resurrection of Jesus Christ, human suffering can be imbued with redemptive meaning. The sick person is no longer a cursed figure, but rather an image of Jesus, the Suffering Servant.

THE CHURCH'S MINISTRY TO THE SICK AND DYING
Jesus' ministry to the sick is continued in his Body, the Church, itself a sign and instrument of the kingdom, a leaven among nations. The Good Samaritan is the model of Christian compassion toward our suffering brothers and sisters (Lk 10:25–37). Jesus goes so far as to identify himself with the sick: "I was sick and you visited me" (Mt 25:36). The patristic Church seems to have grasped this gospel insight and put it into practice. Writing to the community at Philippi in the second century, Bishop Polycarp of Smyrna enjoins the clergy to "keep an eye on all who are infirm."[22] The *Apostolic Tradition* of Hippolytus of Rome speaks of gifts for the sick as well as the consolation derived by a visit to the sick made by the local bishop, "for a sick man is much comforted that the high priest remembered him."[23] This ministry led to the founding of Christian hospitals as early as 369 in Asia Minor by St. Basil, 375 in Edessa by St. Ephraim, and in Rome in the year 400, as well as the foundation of numerous religious communities dedicated to caring for the sick. The very French word for hospital, *Hotel-Dieu* (God's hotel), reflects this concern.

Jesus promised to be present to us "always, to the close of the age" (Mt 28:20). His is a reconciling presence, a ministry of reconciliation entrusted to his Church (2 Cor 5:18–19). The Church's mission in the world is to be a loving, healing, reconciling presence with special concern and affection for the helpless, the sick, the infirm, and the aging. Reflecting the attitude of its founder, the Church's option should always be first of all for the poor and lowly. This overall ministry of reconciliation and healing exerts a prophetic and humanizing influence on social and environmental issues so easily overlooked, such as adequate housing for the poor, a more equitable sharing of food with the hungry, the prevention of drug and alcohol abuse, a better stewardship of natural resources, and nuclear disarmament and the curtailment of the spiraling arms race. The Church's ministry of healing should not be isolated or viewed apart from the rest of its mission to be a visible sign of Christ's continued presence in the world. [24] Christ's commission to his Church to preach the kingdom of God and to heal the sick was a single commission. This ministry to the sick and dying is carried out on three interrelated levels: pastoral, charismatic, and sacramental.

Pastoral Ministry
"Every scientific effort to prolong life and every act of care for the sick, on the part of any person, may be considered a preparation for the Gospel and a sharing in Christ's healing ministry" (no. 32). With this wide-angle vision, the revised rites begin to delineate the Offices and Ministries for the Sick. All Christians by virtue of their baptism participate "by doing all that they can to help the sick return to health, by showing love for the sick, and by celebrating the sacraments with them" (no. 34). Chapter 1, Visits to the Sick, describes the visitation of the sick as a responsibility incumbent not only upon the priests but upon all Christians, with an openness to sharing scripture and prayer with them. The Church's pastoral ministry to the sick is practiced in a more intimate way by the family and friends and all who care for the sick and

dying at home, in the parish, and in hospitals, hospices, and nursing homes. For this reason, the very title of the reformed rites, unlike other sacramental revisions, includes the context of their celebration and ministration. The original English literal translation of the Roman *editio typica, The Rite of Anointing and the Pastoral Care of the Sick,* is now rendered more freely *Pastoral Care of the Sick: Rites of Anointing and Viaticum.* The rites for the sick and dying should always be seen as a sacramental expression of the Church's ongoing pastoral ministry. This pastoral ministry to the sick is not expendable and undergirds any further charismatic or sacramental ministrations.

Charismatic Ministry
The Acts of the Apostles abound with instances of charismatic healing (Acts 6:8; 8:5–11; 10:38; 13:9–12; 14:8–12; 15:12; 10:11–16). There is also strong evidence of a flourishing charismatic ministry in the early Church, as attested to by Quadratus (c. 125), Justin Martyr (d.c. 165), Tatian (c. 160), Irenaeus of Lyon (d.c. 202), Terullian (d.c. 220), and Origen (d.c. 320).[25] Some have attributed the waning of explicit charismatic healing activity to the rejection of the enthusiastic Montanist movement of the Spirit in the second century; others locate the slackening of charisms in a loss of spiritual vitality resulting from the conversion of Constantine and the advent of the cultural synthesis known as "Christendom."[26] Nonetheless, traces of charismatic healing continued in the lives of saints and worthies such as Martin Luther (d. 1546), Philip Neri (d. 1595), George Fox (d. 1691), John Wesley (d. 1791), Pastor Blumhardt (d. 1880), and Father John of Kronstadt (d. 1908).[27] In the Roman Communion, charismatic healing is found in shrines dedicated to the memory of the saints, for example, Mary at Lourdes, and in the provision for verifiable healings required in the canonization process.

Although charismatic healing has therefore always been recognized, at least theoretically, only in this century through the efforts of pentecostal and neo-pentecostal communities has this gift of the Spirit been more fully restored to the Church.

Charismatic and sacramental healing have many similarities. They are situated within the community of the Church, although a healer with a special charism or a presiding liturgical celebrant may play a greater role in the service. They employ similar gestures, namely, the laying on of hands, the sense of touch conceived particularly as a way of bestowing or releasing the power of the Holy Spirit. They are both, charismatic and liturgical, first and foremost prayer: prayer of petition (charismatic "soaking prayer," sacramental "litany of intercession") and prayer of praise and thanksgiving.

Thomas Talley wisely notes that "there has come an increasing blurring of the distinction between the church's liturgical address to affliction and the charism of thaumaturgy, the effecting of miraculous cures, and with that blurring of distinction, a serious confusion regarding the whole nature of sacramental realities."[28] What then is the basis for a distinction between charismatic healing and the sacramental ministry, both of which have a rightful place in the life of the Church? In my opinion, this distinction is made on three grounds: (1) the basis of different modalities of prayer rooted in scriptural origin, (2) their respective place in the Church, and (3) the expected results. First of all, in the New Testament, charismatic healing is mentioned among the charismata listed by Paul in 1 Corinthians 12: gifts of healing and miracles within the community used to build up the Body of Christ. Anointing of the sick finds its scriptural precedent in James 5:14–15, where the elders or presbyters appear to be not simply men of advanced years or wisdom, but rather officeholders or ministers in the primitive Church. As Paul's description of the charismata is to be located within the total picture of his message to the Corinthian community, so likewise it is helpful to recognize the background of James' letter. The author is advocating prayer as a response to various situations in the life of a Christian, be this hardship, good spirits, or sickness—in which case the presbyters are to be summoned.

Second, regarding their respective place in the Church, the Church embraces both charism and sacrament. The sacramental may appear to mirror more the visible, tangible, incarnational side of the Church, whereas the charismatic reflects more the invisible, intangible, pneumatological aspect of the Church. Too great a split or cleavage should be avoided, however, for both come from God and should be animated by the Spirit of Jesus. It follows that charismatic healing partakes of the charismatic dimension just as sacramental healing—in particular, the anointing of the sick—is related to the Church's liturgy on behalf of the sick.

Finally, concerning expectations that are sought from charismatic and sacramental healing, there seems to be a marked disinclination to predict results. Charismatic healing is often not instantaneous, and the grace of anointing the sick is described with a necessary ambiguity. Both involve expectant faith: discernment of the Spirit should also be undertaken as to what the praying community and the sick person can realistically expect. For this reason, for example, several optional prayers are provided in the anointing ritual depending on the condition of the sick Christian. In general, however, one could say that charismatic healing intends a cure, be this physical, psychological ("healing of the memories"), or spiritual (healing from sinful habits such as drug, alcohol, or sexual abuse). Sacramental healing would appear to be less directly concerned with physical or emotional cures, but rather aims at a deeper spiritual conformation with Christ through the healing power of the paschal mystery.[29]

Here are some suggested principles of discernment by which service for the sick, in particular charismatic healing, may be tested:

1. Does the service flow out of the local Christian community's ongoing pastoral care of the sick?
2. Is the prayer service pastorally responsible in terms of prior preparation and follow-up care?
3. Is there a sense of cooperation with the medical profession?
4. Is there a proper emphasis on the worship of God and service of neighbor, rather than a narrowly selfish therapeutic attitude which delights in the "miraculous"?
5. Are healings, whenever and wherever they occur, signs pointing to a deepened faith and conversion in which the beneficiaries become changed or transformed persons?
6. Is the approach imbued with the central mystery of the Christian faith, the passion, death, and resurrection of Jesus Christ and our participation in this saving paschal event?[30]

Sacramental Ministry
We have seen that in a crisis situation when life seems out of control, such as serious illness, we are forced to realize our utter dependence upon God. Jesus has shown us the way through his perfect act of trust and love that the Father would not abandon him. The followers of Jesus, animated by his Spirit, know that the final word about human existence is not death but life, not fear and despair but hope and confidence as children of a loving Father. This is the paschal mystery we celebrate in the sacramental ministry to the sick and dying.

First, liturgical celebrations are not private functions but actions of the Church; hence their communal celebration—which admits of varying degrees—is preferred over the individual and quasi-private administration.[31] Indeed, the notion of Church or faith community belongs intrinsically to any definition of liturgy, which as ritual prayer in community is the official public worship of the Church. All this has profound implications for the public or ecclesial character of the sacramental ministry to the sick and dying. The visitation of the sick need not always be a one-to-one encounter. Chapter 1, Visits to the Sick, provides for a liturgical service which fosters common prayer with and for the sick. The communion of the sick, as first mentioned in the earliest full description of the eucharist from the pen of Justin Martyr in Rome (d. c. 165), should be an extension of the Sunday eucharistic assembly.[32] The sacrament of anointing may now be celebrated communally, even in large assemblies. Viaticum, the sacrament for the dying, is preferably administered in the context of a Mass. And the theology behind the commendation of the dying is that the praying Church accompanies the Christian departing this life as far as it can before entrusting the person into the care of the saints and angels of the Church triumphant of heaven, who welcome and lead him or her to the heavenly throne of God.

The revised rites provide for the emergency situation of Christian Initiation for the Dying in chapter 8: baptism, confirmation, and first eucharist for a dying adult or child. The sacraments for the sick and dying, like all sacraments, build on the foundation of baptism, the gateway sacrament to the Christian life. Illness is a special way of sharing in the paschal mystery, which began for us on the day of our baptism when we first died with Christ and were raised up to a new life (Rom 6:3–11). Death itself is a kind of second baptism. The sign of the cross that began the rites of Christian initiation, and is once again traced on the forehead of a dying Christian, is reminiscent of baptism. The introductory rites at funerals include the Easter candle, the sprinkling of the body with holy water, and the clothing with the white pall. One can apply the initiatory liminal model in a very radical way to Christian existence itself. In this sense, our earthly life is a pilgrimage to God; it is a time of transition marked off by two threshold experiences. Baptism constitutes the first threshold experience in our journey toward God, death is the second. To rephrase the words of Kübler-Ross, in a very real Christian sense, death is the final stage of growing begun at baptism.[33]

The sacrament of penance/reconciliation may also be considered in this context as a means of grace toward reintegrating ourselves to our baptismal commitment. Citing St. Ambrose, the revised *Rite of Penance* states: "The Church possesses both water and tears: the water of baptism, the tears of penance."[34] If some mysterious relationship exists between sin and sickness, it follows correlatively that reconciliation and healing often go together. The close relationship between penance and anointing has been historically further intensified by the association of anointing with deathbed reconciliation during the Middle Ages. All the rites for the sick and dying—communion, anointing, viaticum, continuous rites in exceptional circumstances (penance, anointing, viaticum)—make provision for the sacrament of penance, when desirable or necessary. The Rite for Reconciliation of Individual Penitents is included as an appendix in *Pastoral Care of the Sick*. Oftentimes for a sick Christian, a serious illness may be a conversion experience that finds full expression in the sacrament of penance celebrated as an authentic personal encounter with the risen Christ, the primordial sacrament. In emergencies or other trying pastoral situations, as indicated in the Celebration of Viaticum and Continuous Rite of Penance, Anointing, and Viaticum, the confession may have to be more generic. Often overlooked in the *Rite of Penance* are the model penitential services found in Appendix II. One of these is designed for the sick and bears the title: The Time of Sickness is a Time of Grace. The examination of conscience poignantly depicts the trials of the sick person living out the Christian commitment undertaken at baptism:

"Do I trust God's goodness and providence, even in times of stress and illness?
Do I give in to sickness, to despair, to other unworthy thoughts and feelings?
Do I fill my empty moments with reflections on life and with prayer to God?
Do I accept my illness and pain as an opportunity for suffering with Christ, who redeemed us by his passion?
Do I live by faith, confident that patience in suffering is of great benefit to the Church?
Am I thoughtful of others and attentive to my fellow patients and their needs?
Am I grateful to those who look after me and visit me?
Do I give a good Christian example to others?
Am I sorry for my past sins, and do I try to make amends for them by my patient acceptance of weakness and illness?"[35]

Penance/reconciliation is the healing sacrament directed explicitly toward the forgiveness of postbaptismal sins.

We have already explored the tradition of the sacrament of anointing the sick with blessed oil. Another tactile symbolic action closely associated with the anointing has been the *laying on of hands*.

Norman Cousins relates the experience of a doctor who regularly lays hands on the sick as part of their medical treatment. [36] Furthermore, the last senses to fail us are the sense of hearing and the sense of touch. The imposition of hands is a basic sacramental gesture that figures prominently in all the sacraments: the cathechumenal liturgies, exorcisms, confirmation of the sacraments of initiation; the epiclesis and final blessing of the eucharist; the action that accompanies the prayer of absolution now restored in penance; the central sacramental sign of holy orders; and the blessing at marriages.[37]

In the gospels and Acts, the laying on of hands (touching) is the healing gesture par excellence. Godfrey Diekmann counts eighteen such instances of healing or raising from the dead in Mark's gospel (in twelve instances "touch," six instances of "laying on of hands"); in Matthew, twelve incidents (nine "touch," three "laying on of hands"); in Luke, ten instances (eight "touch," two "laying on of hands").[38] Not only does Jesus heal by touching or the laying of hands on the sick, but the multitudes are also cured by touching him: "And wherever he came, in villages, city, or country, they laid the sick in the market places, and besought him that they might touch even the fringe of his garment; and as many as touched it were made well" (Mk 6:56).

In the tradition of the Church, the laying on of hands has often been associated with the application of the blessed oil. In the early third century, Origen, quoting James 5:14-15, rather spontaneously substitutes "let them lay hands on him" for "let them pray over him," the result being: "let the sick man call the elders of the Church, and let them lay hands on him, anointing him with oil, in the name of the Lord."[39] The rite for anointing the sick in the Ambrosian liturgy of Milan, in sources dating from the ninth and tenth centuries, further indicates that this interpretation could reflect the ritual practice of the early Church. The service, which may involve as many as twelve concelebrating presbyters who anoint the chest, the hands, and the feet, bears the official title *Impositio manuum super infirmum* (The Imposition of Hands on the Sick).[40] One commentator suggests that the laying on of hands could be conceived as a synonym for the anointing of the sick, a case of a part representing the whole, much the same way as the seal (*sphragis*) or enlightenment were ancient synonyms for baptism, or the action of dismissal and blessing (*missa*) gave its name to the Mass.[41]

In this century, the laying on of hands was first restored to the anointing of the sick, then called extreme unction, in the 1952 edition of the *Roman Ritual*, where it accompanied the prayer of exorcism. It is given a much greater emphasis in the revised rites of 1972, where the introductory notes describe the sacrament of anointing as consisting "especially in the laying on of hands by the priests of the Church, the offering of the prayer of faith, and the anointing of the sick with oil made holy by God's blessing" (no. 5). In contrast to confirmation, where the laying on of hands is subsumed into the gesture of anointing with chrism, the anointing rite provides for a more explicit action of imposition by the presbyters in silence, which occurs after the litany of intercession before the blessing/thanksgiving over the oil. The directives for visiting the sick also suggest that the priest conclude the visit by laying hands upon the sick person's head. In the interest of good symbolic actions, the hands should be placed squarely upon the head of the sick person, analogous to the action of the bishop at ordination. Other ministers to the sick are invited to trace the sign of the cross on the sick person's forehead.

As Aquinas noted, all other sacraments are ordered to the *eucharist*.[42] Baptism enables us to participate in a eucharistic community. The eucharist itself is a

sacrament of reconciliation, a sacrifice in which the
healing power of the paschal mystery is applied to the
sick and dying. We have already examined the
tradition of communion of the sick and viaticum in
earlier chapters. What is important for now is to note
the frequent mention of healing in the communion rite.
In one of the two alternative quiet prayers of
preparation for communion, the presider prays that the
eucharist will bring "health in mind and body." The
showing of the consecrated elements is accompanied
by the rephrasing of the centurion's words: "Lord, I
am not worthy . . . but only say the word and I shall
be healed." The gift of viaticum, literally "food for the
journey," is in anticipation of the promise: "He who
eats my flesh and drinks my blood has eternal life, and
I will raise him up on the last day" (Jn 6:54). Finally, as
forthrightly articulated in every major eucharistic
instruction emanating from Rome from 1949 to 1973,
the primary and original reason for reservation of the
eucharist outside Mass is for the administration of
viaticum; the secondary reasons are the giving of
communion and the adoration of the Blessed
Sacrament.[43]

The ministry of the Church to the sick also finds
liturgical expression in the revised Sacramentary,
where special Mass prayers are provided, as well as in
readings from the Lectionary.[44] Furthermore, the most
recent English revision, *Pastoral Care of the Sick*, has
added special intercessions for the sick to be inserted
into Eucharistic Prayers I, II, and III. It also includes a
special preface for the Mass in which the anointing
takes place, the main body of which is as follows:

"In the splendor of his rising
your Son conquered suffering and death
and bequeathed to us his promise
of a new and glorious world,

where no bodily pain will afflict us,
and no anguish of spirit.

"Through your gift of the Spirit,
you bless us even now,
with comfort and healing
strength and hope,
forgiveness and peace.

"In this supreme sacrament of your love
you give us the risen body of your Son:
a pattern of what we shall become
when he returns again at the end of time" (no. 145).

CONCLUSION

We have touched upon some of the theological dimensions of sickness and healing. Sickness is a disruptive experience that afflicts the total person, a crisis of communication with self, with others, and with God. The pain and turmoil that accompany serious illness must be seen within the wider mystery of suffering and evil. A relationship exists between sin and human sickness, both manifestations of evil in the world. Conversely, the promised salvation in Christ Jesus will have holistic ramifications in the resurrection of all flesh. God's redemptive plan unfolds in Jesus' ministry to the sick. His healing works are eschatological signs of the kingdom, proleptic signs of the transforming power of God already at work raising up a fallen world. The ultimate healing transformation, however, comes about through Jesus' death and resurrection. The patient endurance of inevitable illness and physical death as an expression of love and trust is a primordial way every human being participates in this saving paschal mystery that is the Life of the world.

Christ continues his mission of healing and reconciliation in his Body, the Church, a visible sign of his enduring presence in the world. More specifically,

166

the Church's ministry to the sick and dying happens on three interrelated levels: a pastoral ministry, a charismatic ministry, and a sacramental ministry. The pastoral ministry of compassion and outreach to the sick and afflicted is the indispensable basis for the charismatic and sacramental ministries. Charismatic healing has always existed in the Church and is best considered as a ministry distinct from the sacramental ministry, lest an unfortunate confusion result between the two. While charismatic healing generally looks toward the recovery of health, the sacramental ministry celebrates the paschal mystery of Jesus crucified and risen at work in the life of the Christian who is ill.

The sacramental ministry recognizes the ecclesial or communal nature of all liturgical celebrations, including liturgies for the sick. The sacramental ministry to the sick and dying finds expression in the sacraments of Christian initiation (baptism, confirmation, first eucharist), the sacrament of penance/reconciliation, the sacrament of anointing the sick, the sacramental gesture of laying of hands, and the eucharist, considered both as the sacrifice of the Mass and the sacrament reserved for communion of the sick and viaticum. The next chapter will treat more concretely the pastoral praxis of this sacramental ministry.

NOTES

1.   See Mario Alberton, *Un sacrement pour les malades* (Paris: Editions du Centurion, 1978) 27–34. Also M. Jennifer Glen, "Sickness and Symbol: The Promise of the Future," *Worship* 54 (1980) 397–410; Leonard Bowman, *The Importance of Being Sick* (Wilmington, N.C.: Consortium Books, 1976).

2.   J.H. van den Berg, *The Psychology of the Sickbed* (New York: Humanities Press, 1972) 24–26.

3.   Austin Flannery (ed.), *Vatican Council II. The Conciliar and Post Conciliar Documents* (New York: Costello, 1975) 362.

167

4. See also Psalms 26, 28, 32, 38, 49, 51, 69, 88, and 102.

5. Karl Rahner, *On the Theology of Death*, Quaestiones Disputatae 2 (New York: Herder, 1961) 24–34.

6. See John A. Sanford, *Healing and Wholeness* (New York: Paulist, 1977); Morton T. Kelsey, *Prophetic Ministry* (New York: Crossroad, 1982); Bernard J. Tyrrell, *Christotherapy II* (Ramsey, N.J.: Paulist, 1982).

7. A classic study of this phenomenon is Mary Hamilton, *Incubation or the Cure of Diseases in Pagan Temples and Christian Churches* (London, 1906).

8. Victor Frankl, *The Will to Meaning: Foundations and Applications of Logotherapy* (New York: World, 1969).

9. Dennis Linn and Matthew Linn, *Healing of Memories* (New York: Paulist, 1974).

10. See Norman Cousins, *Anatomy of an Illness* (New York: W.W. Norton, 1979).

11. See the insightful reflections of a Jewish rabbi, Harold S. Kushner, *When Bad Things Happen to Good People* (New York: Schocken Books, 1981).

12. Michael Galligan, *God and Evil* (New York: Paulist, 1976), develops these two approaches.

13. See Edward Schillebeeckx, *God the Future of Man* (New York: Sheed & Ward, 1968); Johannes Metz, *Theology of the World* (New York: Herder & Herder, 1969); Jürgen Moltmann, *Theology of Hope* (New York: Harper & Row, 1967).

14. See Jürgen Moltmann, "The 'Crucified God': God and the Trinity Today," in *The God Question*, Concilium vol. 6, no. 8, ed. Johannes B. Metz (London: Burns & Oates, 1972) 26–37.

15. Franz Dölger, "Der Heiland," in *Antike und Christentum* VI, 4. (Münster, 1950) 241–72.

16. Jacques Pasquier, "Healing Relationships," *The Way* 16 (1976) 208–15.

17. Louis Monden, *Signs and Wonders: A Study of the Miraculous Element in Religion* (New York: Desclee, 1966).

18. See R.A. Lambourne, *Community, Church, and Healing* (London: Darton, Longman & Todd, 1963) 33–44. See also James Kallas, *The Significance of the Synoptic Miracles* (London: SPCK, 1961); Alan Richardson, *The Miracle Stories of the Gospels* (London: SCM Press, 1941).

19. I am grateful to H. Boone Porter for this insight.

20. *Constitution on the Sacred Liturgy* para. 7 (Flannery 4–5).

21. *Constitution on the Sacred Liturgy* para. 9, 59 (Flannery 6, 20).

22. *The Epistle of Polycarp to the Philippians*, Early Christian Writings, vol. 6, tr. Maxwell Staniforth (New York: Penguin Books, 1968) 146.

23. Gregory Dix (ed.), *The Apostolic Tradition*, XXX, p. 57.

24. See Bernard Cooke, *Ministry to Word and Sacrament* (Philadelphia: Fortress, 1976) 341–402. This more holistic vision also appears to be the general thrust of the pontificate of John Paul II as evidenced in *Redemptor Hominis* (4 March 1979).

25. This patristic date is examined by Evelyn Frost, *Christian Healing* (London: Mowbray, 1954). See also Morton T. Kelsey, *Healing and Christianity* (New York: Harper & Row, 1973).

26. On the abiding charism of healing in the Church see John V. Taylor, *The Go-Between God. The Holy Spirit as Christian Mission* (Philadelphia: Fortress, 1973) 198–222.

27. Percy Dearmer, *Body and Soul* (London, 1909) 353–400.

28. Thomas Talley, "Healing: Sacrament or Charism?" *Worship* 46 (1972) 520. See also James D.G. Dunn, *Jesus and the Spirit. A Study of the Religious and Charismatic Experience of Jesus and the First Christians as Reflected in the New Testament.* (Philadelphia: Westminster, 1975); Karl Rahner, *The Dynamic Element in the Church* (Freiburg: Herder, 1964) 42–83.

29. For more on charismatic healing see Francis MacNutt, *Healing* (Notre Dame, Ind.: Ave Maria Press, 1974) and its sequel *The Power to Heal* (Notre Dame, Ind.: Ave Maria Press, 1977). See also Rene Laurentin, *Catholic Pentecostalism*

(Garden City, N.Y.: Doubleday, 1977) 100–131; *Theological and Pastoral Orientations on the Catholic Charismatic Renewal. Prepared at Malines, Belgium, May 21–26, 1974.* (Notre Dame, Ind.: Word of Life, 1974) 55–58.

30. Charles W. Gusmer, "I Was Sick and You Visited Me," *Worship* 48 (1974) 516–525. See also *The Church's Ministry of Healing: Report of the Archbishop's Commission* (London: Church).

31. *Constitution on the Sacred Liturgy*, para. 26 (Flannery 10).

32. *First Apology* 67.5, in *Prayers of the Eucharist, Early and Reformed*, ed. R.C.D. Jasper & G.J. Cuming (New York: Oxford University Press, 2nd ed. 1980) 20.

33. Elisabeth Kübler-Ross, *Death, The Final Stage of Growth* (Englewood Cliffs, N.J.: Prentice Hall, 1975) 117–118.

34. *Rite of Penance* para. 2, citing Ambrose, *Letter* 41/12 (PL 16/1116).

35. *Rite of Penance*, Appendix II, para. 68.

36. Cousins, *Anatomy of an Illness* 135.

37. Godfrey Diekmann, "The Laying On of Hands: the Basic Sacramental Rite," The Catholic Theological Society of America, *Proceedings* 29 (1974) 350–51. See also Joseph Coppens, *L'imposition des mains et les rites connexes dans le nouveau testament et dans l'église ancienne* (Paris, 1925) 28–109.

38. Godfrey Diekmann, "The Laying On of Hands in Healing," *Liturgy* 25 (1980) 7–10, 36–38.

39. *On Leviticus*, Hom. 2 (GCS, 29, 295 ff). In Paul F. Palmer, *Sacraments and Forgiveness* Source of Christian Theology, vol. 2 (Westminster, Md.: Newman Press, 1959) 278.

40. See A.M. Triacca, "Le rite de l'impositio manuum super infirmum dans l'ancienne liturgie ambrosienne," in *La maladie et la mort du chrétien dans la liturgie* (Rome: Edizioni Liturgiche, 1975) 339–60.

41. A. Malvy, "Extrême onction et imposition des mains," *Recherches de science religieuse* 7 (1917) 519–23; 22 (1932) 320–24.

42. *Summa Theologica* III, q. 65, a. 3.

43. See S.C. of Sacraments, Instruction *Quam Plurimun*, 1 Oct 1949: AAS 41 (1949), pp. 509–510. The most recent articulation is found in S.C.D.W., *Eucharistiae Sacramentum*, 21 June 1973, no. 5. See also Nathan Mitchell, *Cult and Controversy: The Worship of the Eucharist outside Mass* (New York: Pueblo, 1982).

44. *Sacramentary* 32; *Lectionary*, nos. 871–75.

Chapter Five

Pastoral Praxis

The decrees of Pius X advocating a more frequent
reception of communion took years to become part of
the spirituality and pastoral praxis of the Church. The
revised rites for the sick and dying will probably take a
comparable amount of time to be absorbed fully into
people's consciousness and the Church's ministry to
the sick. Even today one wonders at times if there are
not two sacraments of anointing of the sick: an
anointing that is still too often postponed until the last
moments of life, as if there had been no reform of
extreme unction; and communal anointings that in an
irresponsible manner seem to anoint everything that
moves. Added to this is the compounded confusion
that reigns in some circles over the relationship of the
sacrament of anointing to charismatic healing. This
chapter will be concerned with the overall climate
necessary to implement the rites properly as well as
with their liturgical celebration.

THE OVERALL PASTORAL CLIMATE
In one of the finest essays on the new rite, Adolf
Knauber urged that a new overall pastoral atmosphere
should prevail.[1] Earlier theological manuals spoke of
"adversaries," schools of thought, or movements in
conflict with the stated position. There are also
"adversaries" that would deprive the rites for the sick
and dying of their proper context and pastoral
implementation. These adversaries are a death-

denying culture, misunderstandings regarding the
liturgy, and abuses associated with the last rites.

Death-denying Culture

There is no dearth of literature on the subject of death
and dying. Dr. Elisabeth Kübler-Ross is perhaps the
best known of many authors bringing insight and
compassion to this field. The New York-based
Foundation of Thanatology regularly conducts
symposia on specific topics relating to care for the
dying. Personal account books, plays, and television
documentaries about death and dying abound.[2]
Nevertheless, it is doubtful how much of all this has
filtered down into people's consciousness. At its core,
America is still very much a death-denying society.

Take the example of vocabulary. The medical
profession describes death with such terminology as
"cerebral accident," "cardiovascular accident,"
"circulatory accident." The naive observer could be led
to believe that he or she could go on living forever if
one of these "accidents" did not happen. The
euphemisms of the mortuary business are also well
known: undertakers have become funeral directors,
coffins are caskets, hearses are called coaches, flowers
are renamed floral tributes, corpses even retain their
personal names as if still living.[3] In colloquial speech
we have invented ways to avoid using the word
"death" or "died": a person "passes away," "expires,"
or "passes on."

Another instance of the denial of death is what
Geoffrey Gorer has called the "pornography of death."
Just as repression of human sexuality during the
Victorian era ultimately led to a perverse fascination
with sex and the plague of pornography, so also the
repression of the inevitability of human death has
resulted in a host of movies and books reveling in a

perverse fascination with violent death and gore.[4] Ernest Becker, in his Pulitzer Prize-winning book, *The Denial of Death,* felt that the consciousness of death is the primary repression, not sexuality, as taught by Sigmund Freud. According to Becker, the single greatest task that confronts every human being is to face and accept the inevitability of his or her own death.[5] All of this may lead one to ask: why is it that the two things people are most reluctant to speak about are how we come into the world (human sexuality) and how we leave (human death)?

This death-denying mood finds still another example in the depersonalization of sickness and death. Changing family patterns have contributed in part to this. With greater mobility available today, people are often far removed from the extended family; the emphasis is on the nuclear family without the grandparents and relatives. At the same time, increased longevity has led to the institutionalization of the aging process: nursing homes and retirement villages irreverently scorned by Maggie Kuhn of the Gray Panthers as "human warehouses" and "playpens."[6] This depersonalization of death and dying means that people seldom die at home anymore, unless in the case of sudden and unexpected death. Children especially are more and more totally removed from the dying process.

Why have we allowed this denial of death to happen? The underlying issue seems to be a question of values. Contemporary society idolizes the young, the beautiful, and the healthy. Henri Nouwen has challenged us to realize that being is not the same as having, that self-esteem is not dependent on success, and that goodness is not equatable with popularity.[7] These are but some of the symptoms of the malaise that makes it difficult for Americans to accept fallibility, vulnerability, and finiteness in whatever sphere of human life. Behind this lies the root problem of the lack of an adequate philosophy of life or meaning system capable of integrating the inevitability of death.

Even among professing Christians there is much confusion about the Church's teaching on the afterlife. In 1979, the Vatican Congregation for Sacred Doctrine sought to dispel some of this confusion with a helpful statement summarizing the Catholic tradition on the subject of eschatology. Central to Christian belief is the resurrection of the dead.[8] The whole person will share in the resurrection, for it is "the extension to human beings of the Resurrection of Christ itself." A spiritual element survives after death that is endowed with consciousness and will so that one can say the "human self" subsists: to designate this element, the Church uses the term "soul" as accepted by scripture and tradition. Also reaffirmed are the value of praying for the dead, the "glorious manifestation" of the Lord distinct from the situation of people immediately after death, and the reality of judgment. The document goes on to warn of "arbitrary imaginative representations" of the human situation after death: the images of scripture are to be used in a way that discerns their profound meaning without overdrawing them in such wise as to trivialize the realities designated by the images. Most candid and forthright of all, the Congregation stated: "Neither scripture nor theology provides sufficient light for a proper picture of life after death." On the one hand, through the power of the Holy Spirit, a fundamental continuity exists between our present life in Christ and the future life. On the other hand, there is a radical discontinuity between the two because the dispensation of faith will be replaced by the economy of the fullness of life.

Reflections such as these should find their way into preaching and catechesis, especially at the time of the loss of a loved one and at other appropriate times during the Church year such as the feasts of All Saints and All Souls. Above all, the pastoral minister to the sick and dying must have confronted first of all the unavoidability of his or her own death in order to be present and be of meaningful service to others.

Misunderstandings of Sacramental Theology
What is a priest to do when stopping at the scene of an accident? Should he indiscriminately anoint the injured victim in every instance, just to be sure? Again, when is the best time to administer the sacraments in a hospital? Is the emergency room always the best place, provided there is time to see the patient afterwards? Should the sick be anointed upon every admission to the hospital? From the early abuses of attempting to communicate the dead to the medieval postponement of anointing until the unconscious Christian was no longer capable of sinning, the tradition of the sacramental ministry to the sick and dying has been particularly vulnerable to popular misunderstandings, at times verging on the magical.[9] Thus some comments are in order about the place of the sacraments in the life of the Church, the "thingness" of the sacraments, the meaning of sacramental grace, *ex opere operato* efficacy, and an overly individualistic conception of the sacraments.[10]

One of the strengths of Catholic Christianity is a strong sacramental tradition that is integral to the very being of the Church. Problems occur, however, when sacramental ministry becomes isolated from the rest of the Church's mission, as if the Church were only in existence to provide sacraments to those who seek them. When this occurs, sacraments are viewed in an absolutist manner as the sole vehicle of the salvific plan of God, quite unrelated to a sense of being Church.

To correct such views, one must remember that the primordial sacrament is Jesus Christ himself in his incarnate risen humanity: there is no sacrament unless Christ. The visibility of the risen Lord is continued in the Church, which is a kind of fundamental sacrament. When the Church acts decisively on behalf of the salvation of its members, we have the seven sacraments in the strict sense. But this sacramental activity must be perceived together with a proclamation of the gospel that deals with the ultimate realities of life. There must also be a personal interiorization through faith and conversion, as well as an outward witness of life lived according to gospel values with a social outreach. A lively sense of the Church's rich tradition and a theological reflection of the faith are likewise needed. The necessary institutional dimension must not be allowed to overwhelm the community of faith in whose service institutional forms exist. The sacraments according to this wider vision are the poetic and symbolic expression of what it means to be Church. They are the Church's most intense self-expression and realization, but they do not exhaust the total activity of the Church. The sacramental life of the Christian community will be strong and vibrant to the extent that it is working in tandem with these other dimensions which make up the Church: the proclamation of ultimate realities, personal interiorization, witness of life and mission, consciousness of tradition as a genetic view of the present, theologican reflection, and institutional integration.[11] This means that the liturgical rites for the sick and the dying are not to be seen in isolation but as the sacramental expression of the Church's ongoing pastoral ministry to the sick and the aging.

Another misunderstanding about the sacraments is an excessive object orientation. Rather than water, oil, or bread and wine, we would speak more correctly of a baptismal bath, an anointing with oil, or a eucharistic meal. Sacraments are not things, but sign-acts or symbolic actions that involve earthly elements. Perhaps an overreliance on the Aristotelian matter-form analogy, where the indeterminate matter is specified by the determining words, has reified sacraments and fostered a mechanical approach to them, as if sacraments resulted from simply putting the two together much like constructing a clock or blending a chemical compound. We might speak more accurately of sacraments as graced human actions accompanied by words. The words interpret the action; they are words of faith, the faith of the Church in what it is doing when it celebrates a sacrament. These words are words of prayer. The application here to anointing and communion of the sick should be obvious.

Still another impoverishment caused by conventional sacramental theology has concerned the nature of divine grace, which all too frequently is understood as a kind of spiritual capital that can be "gained" or "lost." An overemphasis on the gift has led to a neglect of the Giver. Divine grace is a way of describing the personal presence of God in our lives, the indwelling of Father, Son, and Spirit, called "uncreated grace" by the scholastic theologians. "Created grace" is the result of this indwelling, what we commonly call sanctifying or habitual grace. In other words, the Giver deserves the primacy over the gift that enables and brings about this divine indwelling of the Trinity. Moreover, grace is not restricted only to the sacraments.

Karl Rahner has written of a "Copernican revolution" in the sacraments.[12] In the past, sacraments were sometimes thought to be the sole media by which grace was encountered, oases in an otherwise barren secular desert in which God was absent. We have now come to see that human experience itself is already fundamentally and inchoatively graced. All people have been called to share in a life of communion with God. Sacraments express and frame this already existing, if inchoate, religious experience of God. At the same time, the celebration of the sacraments prolongs, enlarges, and intensifies this experience in ways similar to what the Council of Trent had in mind when the Council Fathers said that sacraments confer grace. Paragraph 7 of the *Constitution of the Sacred Liturgy* captures aptly the interaction of these causative and significative moments: "In the liturgy the sanctification of the human person is signified by signs perceptible to the senses and is effected in a way which corresponds to each of these signs." The sacraments are thus normatively the ritual conclusion of a process of transformation. The sacraments express what is already happening, the pouring out of the love of God in Christian initiation, reconciliation, vocational choices, serious illness, and so on. They complete the process and give the experience a new dimension of reality: the sacraments are ritual transformations of religious experience.

One of the hallmarks of Catholic sacramental theology since the Council of Trent has been its emphasis on *ex opere operato* efficacy. The Council Fathers found in this term a common denominator with which to react to the extremes of the Protestant *sola fides* position, as if the sacraments were effective only because of the faith response of the subject. All too often, post-Tridentine manual theology erroneously interpreted the *opus operatum* in a mechanistic, automatic fashion. The original and proper understanding of *opus operatum* efficacy is that it is a strong statement about the priority of grace, the initiative of God in the sacraments; before anything else, the sacraments are actions of Christ. Rather than pitting the *opus operatum*, the objective element, against the *opus operantis*, the subjective element, the two should be seen as complementary aspects of the sacramental encounter, not as contending or conflicting parts of it. The *opus operatum* refers to the divine and objective efficacy of the sacraments: sacraments are effective signs of grace. They are intrinsically efficacious signs of the divine transforming Presence that will reach their goal unless we frustrate the designs of God by putting obstacles in the way. The *opus operantis* refers to the graced human response and involvement: sacraments are also signs of faith. They call forth a mutual and covenantal presence implying conversion and commitment on our part. Not the least of the merits of the Second Vatican Council is its elucidation of a sacramental theology underpinning liturgical renewal, so that as far as possible the celebration of the sacraments may be seen as a dialogical graced human encounter with the mystery of God. [13] For this reason, the revised rites have urged the earliest possible moment for anointing in the case of serious illness and for viaticum when the danger of death *begins* to be present.

A final misconception about the sacraments has been to reduce them to a one-on-one transaction between the designated minister and the subject or recipient. This overly individualistic approach fails to see that it is the Church, the assembled worshipping community, that celebrates the sacraments. *The Constitution on the Sacred Liturgy* prefers the communal celebration of all the sacraments whenever possible; the introductions to the revised rites always contain an extended treatment of Offices and Ministries beginning with the baptized priesthood of the faithful. As a result, the Christian community itself has been restored as the subject of all liturgical celebrations. The priest is more properly called the presiding celebrant, for all the participants are celebrants according to a diversity of roles and ministries. In short, the celebration of the sacraments affects the whole Church. One might say further that the specific quality of *sacramental* grace, as distinct from grace everywhere offered and made available, is a relationship to the Church as the fundamental sacrament in Christ. It is not solely a question of something happening to the individual, but of something happening to the Church, the faith community. It is generally a reciprocal exchange. To take the example of anointing the sick, in the words of the *Constitution on the Church*, "the whole Church commends those who are ill to the suffering and glorified Lord that he may raise them up and save them." In return, the sick are enjoined "to contribute to the good of the People of God by freely uniting themselves to the passion and death of Christ."[14]

Abuses Associated with the "Last Rites"
It is no exaggeration to say that anointing of the sick has been the most misunderstood, most uncommunal, and most unliturgical of the seven sacraments of the Church. The sacrament of anointing continues to be misunderstood by those who for one reason or another continue to use the terms "extreme unction" or "last rites," or in an even more unconscious way by those who fatalistically regard the sacrament as a kind of religious pronouncement of death. Anointing has been the most uncommunal of sacraments: in the past, the family often felt compelled to leave the sick room, perhaps confusing the occasion of anointing with discretion required for sacramental confession. Anointing has been the most unliturgical of sacraments: we are still not far removed in time from priests darting into sickrooms for a quick dabbing with oil.

Here are some positive recommendations that might obviate these abuses and secure a pastoral climate conducive for the rites for the sick and dying, in particular the anointing of the sick. The present revision of rites embodied in *Pastoral Care* should precipitate a renewed catechesis on the basis of the initial pastoral experience and the updating of any existing programs or available materials. The bishop might preside at communal anointings from time to time to lend his support as head of the diocese to the proper implementation of the rites and the pastoral care of the sick.

The emergency room of a hospital is no place to embark on an extended catechesis on the sacraments. Catechesis on ministering to the sick and dying belongs to the mainstream of the Church's preaching and teaching. Parishes might emphasize the Sunday Lectionary readings that afford an occasion to preach on the Church's ministry to the sick, for example, a healing gospel, as well as on the mystery of death. The general intercessions should regularly include a petition for the sick of the parish, who could be mentioned by name. In parishes where this has already become a regular practice, people will ordinarily volunteer the names of their sick relatives and friends. The parish bulletin is an ideal place to advertise the availability and desire of the priests and other ministers to visit and bring communion to the sick. Adult education programs would have more than enough material to focus on: clinical pastoral education, a team concept of ministering to the sick, the emergence of eucharistic ministers and ministries to the sick, the care of the dying, the hospice movement, and so on. These programs should include not only instruction, but also actual practice or field experience, lest they degenerate into a merely academic exercise.

Already in the seventh century, the Mozarabic or Old Spanish liturgy included a cathedral or parish office for the sick comprising both morning and evening prayer. [15] Today when the Liturgy of the Hours is being restored as a participated communal prayer, the intercessions could always mention the sick and the dying. The blessing of throats on the feast of St. Blase might be revitalized by incorporating it into a healing service with intercessory prayers for those ill from physical, mental, or psychological disorders. The visitation of the sick and aging, the most neglected people in contemporary society, could be intensified by choosing special seasons of the year such as Lent as a time to begin. Deacons in particular could be entrusted with the organization of the ministry to the sick. Young people should also be included in this apostolic outreach, perhaps as some form of Christian mission and service preparing for confirmation. A fortiori, catechumens preparing for the sacraments of Christian initiation could "learn how to work actively with others to spread the Gospel and build up the Church" by ministering to the infirm.[16]

Communion of the sick is now more flexible than the monthly First Fridays. Indeed, many shut-ins today are becoming used to a more frequent reception of holy communion and sorely miss the sacrament of the Lord's body and blood in their lives. The selection and formation of eucharistic ministers skilled in visiting the sick could enormously facilitate a more regular eucharistic sharing, especially effective when they are dismissed and sent forth from the table of the Sunday eucharistic assembly. The role of the priest or deacon who animates and coordinates these ministries is more important than ever. Now as before, an important yardstick in measuring pastoral zeal has always been the degree of fidelity in caring for the sick and dying.

Hospitals are special places for exercising the ministry to the sick and the dying. Insofar as a lamentable ignorance is still found among hospital personnel, even in Catholic hospitals, about the Church's revised rites, this would provide a fertile ground for continued catechesis. The catechesis could endeavor to develop a sense of spirituality and motivation among those involved in the caring professions. Doctors need to be reassured that the death of a patient does not constitute a failure or professional setback. Nurses may be overwhelmed by the daily confrontation with pain, suffering, and death. Families who make many personal sacrifices to care for their loved ones also need the encouragement of the Church. Doctors, nurses, family members, and friends all participate in the ministry of Christ to the sick as continued in his Church. John Burke has written that the eucharist is what constitutes the unique identity of a Catholic health-care facility. A Catholic hospital is a eucharistic community: "Eucharistic as all-encompassing—word believed, doctrine taught, people formed, and rite celebrated."[17] Attention might be given to the reverent and dignified celebration of the sacraments of the sick in hospitals. Questions such as these might be posed: What is the best time of the day for the fruitful reception of the eucharist? How can the patients be properly disposed in faith for the celebration of anointing? Are there other religious services that might be provided? The most refined scientific medicine and technology has little value if we have lost the meaning of life, of suffering and death, which is what the sacraments celebrate.

Finally, the best catechesis for any sacrament is always a well-done liturgical celebration: the participation of all the available ministers, the verbal and nonverbal symbols with their inherent power speaking for themselves. As far as possible, the rites for the sick should be seen and celebrated in a communal way as sacraments of the Church, even if this means gathering just a handful of the hospital personnel and family as a praying group. Larger-scale communal anointings of the sick have proven most helpful, given prior catechetical preparation and liturgical planning. Communal anointings may be celebrated in hospitals or in parishes. As for hospitals, these communal anointings seem to work out best in institutions of long-term care or in nursing homes where the people can be more easily assembled. Parishes should provide for communal anointing of their sick parishioners

particularly during the seasons of Advent and
Christmas, Lent and Easter, as well as during the
Ordinary Time of the Church year, when the weather
is usually more favorable.

LITURGICAL CELEBRATION: IS IT *WORSHIP*?
The introduction of clinical pastoral education in
hospitals has greatly improved communication and
counseling skills in ministering to the sick and dying.
In the wake of this development, an immediate
reaction to the traditional sacramental approach of the
Roman Catholic Communion sometimes results in a
bias on the part of pastoral ministers against
sacraments and liturgy with the sick. A healthy sign
toward a recovery of a more balanced view has been
the gradual rediscovery of the value of good ritual in
pastoral care.[18] We are speaking here of Christian
religious ritual, which is how our sacraments and
liturgy communicate. Is it WORSHIP? This handy
mnemonic device spells out some characteristics that
go into good liturgy.[19]

Wholeness in Relationship to the Mission of the Church
Is there a relationship between the sacrament
celebrated and the Church's ministry to the sick as
practiced in parishes and institutions? Are the
sacramental ministrations integrated into this pastoral
ministry as its liturgical expression and transformation?

Wholeness in this sense is understood as a greater
sense of ecclesial unity and integration in which the
ministry to the sick and infirm make up an intrinsic
part of parochial life. Communal anointings can often
be an impetus toward an intensified ministry to the
sick. The ecclesial values inherent in all the rites for the
sick and dying are twofold. There is, first of all, a
personal experience of solidarity with the Church
acting as a caring and compassionate community. For
example, through the anointing of the sick, a bond is

created between the Church and the suffering brothers and sisters; the eucharist as communion or viaticum is always the sacrament of the unity of the Church. Second, the celebration endeavors to bring about a personal experience of dignity and worth: sick people have something to offer and give. We can learn from the patience of the sick and from the wisdom of the old; there is a mutuality of ministry.

Organization
In light of previous pastoral praxis, it seems odd to hear of the need for planning the liturgical celebrations with the sick, be this a visit to the sick, communion of the sick, or the sacrament of anointing (nos. 55, 72, 100). Ideally, the planning could include the sick person and family. Anointing services involving large congregations demand an even greater investment of time and energy. Prior catechesis should be given to the entire parish on the meaning of illness in salvation history, the grace of anointing, and the parish's ministry to the sick and afflicted. This preparation can be imparted by preaching at Sunday Mass, handouts and bulletins, Bible vigils, and services of common prayer.

As far as possible, those who are to be anointed should be known to the pastoral ministers and prepared in advance. The list of communion calls is a good way to begin extending invitations; other people who come forward should be identified in order to follow up the service with continued pastoral care. Transportation will be needed to bring the shut-ins to the church. This prior organization also includes the planning of the liturgical details of celebration: whether or not the anointing is to take place during Mass, the selection of readings, and the choice of other options. A rehearsal might be useful for the various ministers to walk through the rite. Comments should be prepared to the extent that they enable the participants to enter more fully into the mystery celebrated.

Ritual
The worship of the Church should be a sensuous, evocative, moving, humanly attractive religious experience. In other words, it should be good ritual involving the total person: body, mind, heart, imagination, memory, emotions, and feelings. Attention needs to be directed to the liturgical environment. To begin with, the church building itself should be completely accessible to handicapped persons. In a communal anointing, the sick should be seated up front. If need be, alternating pews can be left open for easy access for the laying on of hands and the anointing. The rite of blessing and sprinkling with holy water at the beginning may serve to recall our baptismal relationship to Christ and his Church, just as communion at the close of the service relates the sick person to the Church as a table fellowship of all in Christ. The font and the table are the twin pillars of the Church's sacramental system to which all the other sacraments are related. A booklet might be provided for the occasion using large type that is easily legible and incorporating devotional elements and readings for use by the sick afterwards as a kind of remembrance and ongoing support. Even in individual anointings, the symbols should speak for themselves: the liturgical vesture, ritual books, vessels for oil, pyxes, corporals, and so on. More than words themselves, the nonverbal features of ritual worship strike deeply into the unconscious mind and leave a lasting impression.

Sharing or Inclusiveness
Full, active conscious participation has been the primary goal of all liturgical renewal from the start.[20] Why should the sacraments for the sick and dying be

an exception? For the sick person, this implies the earliest possible time for anointing so that he or she may experience the sacrament as a true prayer of faith, as it is intended to be; the same holds true for communion and viaticum. The participation at communal anointings should be representative of the entire parish. A convenient time should be chosen for the anointing, perhaps at Sunday Mass. A reception with light refreshments or even a meal provided by parish groups could follow the service to encourage the bonds of friendship among the anointed themselves as well as with the parishioners. The doctors and nurses could be on hand to lend their prayerful support and to reassure the sick and their families in the unlikely event of an emergency. Along with the family and friends, the sick might be asked to present the gifts at Mass. The parish choir may support the singing of the community. Young people should be on hand for their own sake, as well as for the sake of the sick and the elderly: they might serve as ministers of hospitality or ushers along with the other regular ministers of the parish. Retired priests and sisters who live in the area should also be invited. One flaw endemic to all the revised sacramental liturgies is the still impoverished level of participation of the congregation within the celebration itself. We must look for words and gestures to include them more in the actual celebration.

Harmonious Balance

Any sacramental ministration to the sick should be carefully adapted to the condition of those sick and elderly who tire easily and whose attention span is short. The ideal would be a balance between celebration and contemplation, between festivity and silent prayer. This might be the place to comment on that form of participation that most enhances liturgical celebration, namely music and song. There is only scant mention of music in the revised rites, yet the mood-evoking and healing power of music is a known fact, attested to in the earliest full ritual for anointing that took place within the framework of a choral office. (no. 108).[21] In addition to the usual key places for singing at Mass, such as the responsorial psalm, gospel acclamation, and eucharistic acclamations, the rhythm of the celebration would call for a further acclamation or hymn of thanksgiving to be sung after the anointing. The type of music selected for communal anointings should be reassuring and comforting, yet not lugubrious; festive with praise and thanksgiving, but not rambunctious. The use of psalms with their strong evocative power might be particularly helpful. There is also a place for traditional music, which older people might appreciate more.

Integrity of Form
The three elements that make up the sacrament of the sick are (1) the laying on of hands by the presbyters, (2) the prayer of faith, and (3) the anointing with blessed oil. Each of these has an integrity of form to be respected. The laying on of hands should be done in silence with both hands placed firmly on the head of the sick person. The prayer of faith—concentrated especially in the litany of intercession and the prayer of anointing—should avoid any semblance of routine recitation and be as reverent and faith-filled as possible. The blessing or thanksgiving prayer might be said over the oil, which should be kept in a worthy vessel in liquid form without cotton, in contrast to the usual minute oil stocks that disappear into the palm of the hand. The anointing on the forehead and hands or other places should be ample and need not be removed. Eucharistic communion should be provided under both kinds with enough eucharistic ministers on hand to extend the cup.

Prayer

Prayer is the most important single feature of any liturgical celebration. The revised rites for the sick and dying are most insistent on its priority. All of God's people are urged to pray for and with the sick when visiting them. In all the rites, a reading of God's word has been restored in order to dispose the person to receive the sacramental ministration in faith. The anointing is a sacrament of faith to be administered at the beginning of a serious impairment resulting from sickness or old age. Viaticum, with its enriched liturgical format, also calls for an earlier celebration so that the dying Christian can enter more fully into this sacrament of the eucharist given as food for the paschal journey home. Of the scriptural accounts touching sacraments as we know them, the prescription of James for anointing is explicit about the prayer of faith. With the recovery of anointing as a sacrament for the sick, only now are we in a position to appreciate the true power and meaning of this sacrament.

CONCLUSION

Liturgical celebrations express and frame a given experience. In the rites for the sick and dying, this experience is the paschal mystery of Jesus crucified and risen at work in the life of Christians who are seriously ill. The pastoral praxis of these sacraments must first of all create an improved atmosphere that will capture more adequately the meaning of the experience. This pastoral climate must clear the air of the prevailing death-denying mood of contemporary culture, to dispel misunderstandings about sacramental theology, and to correct abuses associated with "extreme unction" and "last rites."

Liturgical celebrations also intensify and enlarge the experience they create. The rites for the sick and dying are efficacious symbols that deepen and transform the paschal mystery relived in the afflicted and infirm. In order for this to happen, the sacraments must be celebrated properly. We have advanced seven criteria for good worship and applied them to the sacramental ministry to the sick: ecclesial Wholeness, Organization or planning, robust Ritual actions, Sharing or inclusiveness, an Harmonious balance, Integrity of form, and a Prayerful spirit that envelops and pervades the entire liturgy.

On December 22, 1982, the National Conference of Catholic Bishops of the United States received the decree of the Sacred Congregation for the Sacraments and Divine Worship, dated December 11, 1982, confirming the approval of *Pastoral Care of the Sick: Rites of Anointing and Viaticum.* The First Sunday of Advent, November 27, 1983, is the effective date for implementing the revised ritual.[22] The Canadian Catholic bishops have already published their own edition with an appendix of prayers for use in Canada.[23] These supplementary texts include prayer before and after reading scripture, in time of sickness, for the dying, for the dead, various blessings (for example, for ministers for the sick, hospitals or clinics, homes for special care), and thanks and praise. There is even a simple blessing of oil for the sick, not to be confused with the sacrament of anointing. This custom reaches back into the early centuries of the tradition of anointing and continues a practice of nonsacramental anointings by lay people that was still provided for in the *Rituale Romanum* of 1614.[24]

In a related development, the new Code of Canon Law (January 25, 1983) treats the anointing of the sick in three chapters pertaining respectively to the celebration of the sacrament, the minister, and the recipients.[25] For the most part, the ten canons reiterate the salient features of the *praenotanda* or introduction to the anointing ritual. The most noteworthy canon, however, is one which did not appear in the 1981 draft revision and thus came as a surprise. There are strong indications that Pope John Paul II may have inserted canon 1002 during the final revision of the document. Canon 1002 of the new Code of Canon Law endorses communal anointings of the sick who have been properly prepared and disposed. This canon *de jure* recognizes what has become *de facto* a regular feature in the life of many parishes. This recognition and endorsement of communal anointings by Church law is far removed from the privatized extreme unction of the pre-Vatican II Church. All these signposts augur well for an even brighter future for a sacramental ministry that brings the strength and consolation of Jesus Christ to the sick.

NOTES

1. Adolf Knauber, *Pastoral Theology of the Anointing of the Sick* (Collegeville, Minn.: Liturgical Press, 1975) 33A–35 A. See also National Conference of Catholic Bishops, "Pastoral Letter on Health and Healing," *Origins* 11:25 (3 December 1981) 396–402. Also valuable readings on the Church's pastoral care of the sick are *The Ministry of Healing: Readings in the Catholic Health Care Ministry* (St. Louis: The Catholic Health Association, 1981) and a special issue of *Liturgy* 2 (1982) devoted to "Ministries to the Sick."

2. The following are but a sampling of available literature on this subject: Doris Lund, *Eric* (New York: Dell, 1974); Herbert Conley, *Living and Dying Gracefully* (Ramsey, N.J.: Paulist, 1977); Stanley Keleman, *Living Your Dying* (New York: Random House, 1974); Ted Rosenthal, *How Could I Not Be Among You?* (New York: Avon Books, 1973); Stewart Alsop, *Stay of Execution* (New York: Lippincott, 1973).

3. Jessica Mitford, *The American Way of Death* (New York: Simon & Schuster, 1963).

4. Geoffrey Gorer, *Death, Grief, and Mourning* (Garden City, N.Y.: Doubleday, 1965).

5.   Ernest Becker, *The Denial of Death* (New York: Knopf, 1973).

6.   Dieter Hessel (ed.), *Maggie Kuhn on Aging* (Philadelphia: Westminister Press, 1977).

7.   Henri Nouwen and Walter Gaffney, *Aging* (New York: Doubleday, 1974).

8.   "Concerning Eschatology," (17 May 1979), as translated and reprinted in the English edition of *L'Osservatore Romano*, 23 July 1979.

9.   See Robert T. Trotter and Juan Antonio Chavira, *Curanderismo: Mexican American Folk Healing* (Athens: University of Georgia Press, 1981).

10.   The following insights are drawn from contemporary sacramental theologians: Edward Schillebeeckx, *Christ the Sacrament* (New York: Sheed & Ward, 1963); Karl Rahner, *The Church and the Sacraments* (New York: Herder, 1963); R. Vaillancourt, *Toward a Renewal of Sacramental Theology* (Collegeville, Minn.: Liturgical Press, 1979); Regis Duffy, *Real Presence* (New York: Harper & Row, 1982).

11.   David Power, "A Theological Perspective on the Persistence of Religion," *Concilium* (new series) 1:9 (Jan 1973) 91–105. I am grateful to Robert Taft for his insight into tradition as a "genetic view of the present."

12.   Karl Rahner, "Secular Life and the Sacraments: A Copernican Revolution," *The Tablet* (London) 6 and 13 March 1971, 236–38, 267–68; "How to Receive a Sacrament and Mean It," *Theology Digest* 19 (1971) 227–34; "Considerations on the Active Role of the Person in the Sacramental Event," *Theological Investigations* 14, trans. D. Burke (New York: Seabury, 1976) 161–84.

13.   Cyprian Vagaggini is generally credited with restoring to liturgical theology this dialogical understanding whereby the sacraments comprise both sanctification and worship. See C. Vagaggini, *Theological Dimensions of the Liturgy* (Collegeville, Minn.: Liturgical Press, 1976). See also Piet Fransen, "Sacraments, Signs of Faith," *Worship* 37 (1962) 31–50.

14.   *Constitution on the Church*, para. 11.

15.   J. Pinell, "The Votive Office of the Sick in the Spanish Rite," in *Temple of the Holy Spirit: Sickness and Death of the Christian in the Liturgy* (New York: Pueblo, 1983).

16.   RCIA, para. 19.

17.   John Burke, "Eucharistic Health Care Facility Transcends Professionalism,," in *The Ministry of Healing* 40.

18.   William H. Willimon, *Worship as Pastoral Care* (Nashville, Tenn.: Abingdon, 1979); H.P.V. Renner, "The Use of Ritual in Pastoral Care," *Journal of Pastoral Care* 33 (1979) 164–74. On the recovery of the sacramental dimension of Church life, see Philip J. Murnion, "A Sacramental Church," *America* (26 March 1983) 226–28.

19.   Charles Gusmer, "Is It Worship? Evaluating the Sunday Eucharist," *Living Worship* vol. 14, no. 10 (1978).

20.   *Constitution on the Sacred Liturgy*, para. 14.

21.   See also the Carolingian Anointing Rite (PL 78:231–36) described in chapter 1 of this book.

22.   Bishops' Committee on the Liturgy, *Newsletter* 19 (1983) 2.

23.   *Pastoral Care of the Sick. Rites of Anointing and Viaticum* (Ottawa: Canadian Conference of Catholic Bishops, 1983).

24.   Ibid. pp. 348–49. See *Rituale Romanum*, tit. IX, cap. VII, 8.

25.   *Codex Iuris Canonici* auctoritate Ioannis Pauli PP II Promulgatus (Libreria Editrice Vaticana, 1983), canons 998–1007 (pp. 177–78).

Appendix A

Liturgical History
of the Sacrament of Anointing

The chart on page 196 showing the history of the sacrament of anointing is intended not as a statistical graph but as a pictorial diagram to illustrate an extremely complex subject.

The first column presents the history of anointing to A.D. 800, when "the sacrament was held above all to be a rite of healing."

The second column sets out (1) the association of anointing and viaticum, and (2) the association of anointing and "death-bed" penance.

The third column shows (1) the practice of public penance and its eventual association with the rite of anointing, and (2) the origins of private penance.

This visual aid is adapted from a supplement that appeared in Placid Murray's "The Liturgical History of the Sacrament of Extreme Unction," in *The Furrow*, vol. 11, September 1960, pp. 572–93, which was based on the work of A. Chavasse, *Étude sur l'onction des infirmes dans l'Eglise latine du IIIe au X^{ie} siecle.*

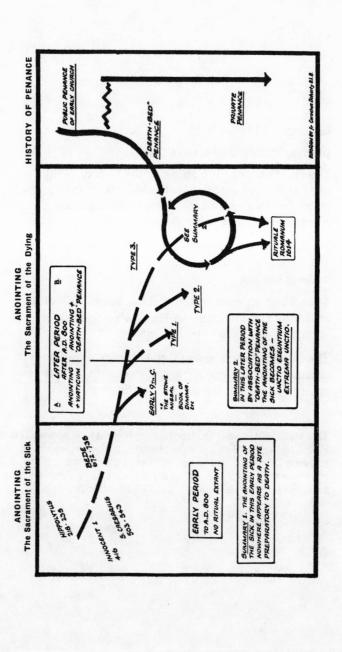

Rite for Sending Special Ministers of Communion Forth from Mass

1. During the breaking of the bread the special ministers of communion come to the altar and place the eucharist in their pyxes.

2. The pyxes are left on the altar during the distribution of communion (and remain there when the eucharist is reposed in the tabernacle).

3. When all stand following the period of thanksgiving after communion, the ministers take the pyxes from the altar and stand facing the celebrant who addresses the congregation in these or similar words: "The special ministers of communion will take the eucharist to those who are confined to their
    have celebrated,

4. Then, using these or similar words, the celebrant addresses the special ministers of communion:

"As you go, take with you not only the sacrament we
    have celebrated,
but also the word of God which we have heard,
as well as the affection of this parish community,
and ask for the prayers of those whom you visit in
    return;
and now let us pray."

5. The Prayer after Communion follows.

6. The ministers depart in silence after the "Amen" to the Prayer after Communion.

7. When the special ministers of communion have left the assembly the announcements are made and the Concluding Rite follows

Reprinted courtesy of Newark Archdiocesan Worship Office.

Appendix C

Pope Addresses Communal Celebration

(On May 28, 1982 Pope John Paul II presided at a communal celebration of the anointing of the sick in Saint George's Cathedral in Southwark, London. The following is the Vatican text of the homily which the Holy Father preached on that occasion.)

My brothers and sisters,

1.   Praised be Jesus Christ. Praised be Jesus Christ who invites us to share in his life through our baptism. Praised be Jesus Christ who calls us to unite our sufferings to his so that we may be one with him in giving glory to the Father in heaven.

Today I greet you in the name of Jesus. I thank all of you for the welcome you have given me. I want you to know how I have looked forward to this meeting with you, especially with those of you who are sick, disabled, or infirm. I myself have had a share of suffering and I have known the physical weakness that comes with injury and sickness.

2.   It is precisely because I have experienced suffering that I am able to affirm with ever greater conviction what St. Paul says in the second reading: "Neither death, nor life, nor angels, nor principalities, nor things present, nor things to come, nor powers, nor height, nor depth, nor anything else in all creation, will be able to separate us from the love of God in Christ Jesus Our Lord" (Rom 8:38–39).

Dear friends, there is no force or power that can block God's love for you. Sickness and suffering seem to contradict all that is worthy, all that is desired by man. And yet no disease, no injury, no infirmity can ever deprive you of your dignity as children of God, as brothers and sisters of Jesus Christ.

3. By his dying on the cross, Christ shows us how to make sense of our suffering. In his passion we find the inspiration and strength to turn away from any temptation to resentment and grow through pain into new life.

Suffering is an invitation to be more like the Son in doing the Father's will. It offers us an opportunity to imitate Christ who died to redeem mankind from sin. Thus, the Father has disposed that suffering can enrich the individual and the whole Church.

4. We acknowledge that the anointing of the sick is for the benefit of the whole person. We find this point demonstrated in the liturgical texts of the sacramental celebration: "Make this oil a remedy for all who are anointed with it; heal them in body, in soul and in spirit, and deliver them from every affliction."

The anointing is therefore a source of strength for both the soul and the body. The prayer of the Church asks that sin and the remnants of sin be taken away (cf. Ds 1969). It also implores a restoration of health, but always in order that bodily healing may bring greater union with God through the increase of grace.

In her teaching on this sacrament, the Church passes on the truth contained in our first reading from St. James: "Is any among you sick? Let him call for the elders of the church and let them pray over him, anointing him with oil in the name of the Lord; and the prayer of faith will save the sick man, and the Lord will raise him up; and if he has committed sins, he will be forgiven" (Jas 5:14–15).

5. This sacrament should be approached in a spirit of great confidence, like the leper in the gospel that has just been proclaimed.

Even the desperateness of the man's condition did not stop him from approaching Jesus with trust. We too must believe in Christ's healing love and reaffirm that nothing will separate us from that love. Surely Jesus wishes to say: "I will; be clean" (Mt 8:3); be healed; be strong; be saved.

My dear brothers and sisters, as you live the passion of Christ, you strengthen the Church by the witness of your faith. You proclaim by your patience, your endurance, and your joy the mystery of Christ's redeeming power. You will find the crucified Lord in the midst of your sickness and suffering.

6. As Veronica ministered to Christ on his way to Calvary, so Christians have accepted the care of those in pain and sorrow as privileged opportunities to minister to Christ himself. I commend and bless all those who work for the sick in hospitals, residential homes, and centers of care for the dying. I would like to say to you doctors, nurses, chaplains, and all other hospital staff: yours is a noble vocation. Remember it is Christ to whom you minister in the sufferings of your brothers and sisters.

7. I support with all my heart those who recognize and defend the law of God which governs human life. We must never forget that every person, from the moment of conception to the last breath, is a unique child of God and has a right to life. This right should be defended by the attentive care of the medical and nursing professions and by the protection of the law. Every human life is willed by our heavenly Father and is part of his loving plan.

No state has the right to contradict moral values which are rooted in the nature of man himself. These values are the precious heritage of civilization. If society begins to deny the worth of any individual or to subordinate the human person to pragmatic or utilitarian considerations, it begins to destroy the defenses that safeguard its own fundamental values.

8.   Today I make an urgent plea to this nation. Do not neglect your sick and elderly. Do not turn away from the handicapped and the dying. Do not push them to the margins of society. For if you do, you will fail to understand that they represent an important truth. The sick, the elderly, the handicapped, and the dying teach us that weakness is a creative part of human living, and that suffering can be embraced with no loss of dignity. Without the presence of these people in your midst you might be tempted to think of health, strength, and power as the only important values to be pursued in life. But the wisdom of Christ and the power of Christ are to be seen in the weakness of those who share his sufferings.

Let us keep the sick and the handicapped at the center of our lives. Let us treasure them and recognize with gratitude the debt we owe them. We begin by imagining that we are giving to them; we end by realizing that they have enriched us.

May God bless and comfort all who are sick. And may Jesus Christ, the savior of the world and healer of the sick, make his light shine through human weakness as a beacon for us and for all mankind. Amen.

Reprinted from Bishops' Committee on the Liturgy, *Newsletter* XVIII (1982) 22–23.

Bibliography

SOURCES

Acta Synodalia sacrosancti concilii oecumenici Vaticani II. Vatican
City: Typis Polyglottis Vaticanis, 1970.

Andrieu, Michel (ed.). *Les Ordines Romani du haut moyen age,* 5
vols. Louvain: Spicilegium Sacrum Lovaniense 11, 23, 24, 28,
29: 1931–1961.

Bishops' Committee on the Liturgy. *Study Text 2: Anointing
and the Pastoral Care of the Sick.* Washington, D.C.: USCC
Publications.

*The Church's Ministry of Healing: Report of the Archbishops'
Commission* (Anglican). London: Church Information Office,
1958.

Codex Iuris Canonici auctoritate Ionnis Pauli PP. II
promulgatus. Vatican City: Libreria Editrice Vaticana, 1983.

Collectio Rituum. The 1964 English Ritual. Collegeville, Minn.:
Liturgical Press, 1964.

Denzinger H. and A. Schönmetzer (eds.). *Enchiridion
Symbolorum. Definitionum et Declarationum.* Freiburg: Herder,
35th ed. 1967.

Dix, Gregory (ed.). *The Apostolic Tradition.* London: SPCK,
1968.

Early Christian Writings. The Apostolic Fathers. Trans. Maxwell
Staniforth. New York: Penguin Books, 1968.

Die griechischen christlichen Schriftsteller der ersten Jahrhunderte.
Ed. Deutsche Akademie der Wissenschaften zu Berlin. Berlin:
Akademie Verlag, 1897.

Flannery, Austin (ed.). *Vatican Council II. The Conciliar and Post Conciliar Documents.* Northport, N.Y.: Costello, 1975.

Hapgood, Isabel F. (ed.). *Service Book of the Holy Orthodox-Catholic Apostolic Church.* Englewood, N.J.: Antiochian Orthodox Christian Archdiocese, 5th ed. 1975

Jasper, R.C.D. and G.J. Cuming (eds.). *Prayers of the Eucharist: Early and Reformed.* New York: Oxford University Press, 1980.

Mansi, J.D. (ed.). *Sacrorum conciliorum nova et amplissima collectio,* 31 vol. Florence-Venice, 1757–1798; reimpression and continuation, Paris, Leipzig, and Arnheim, 1901–1927.

Migne, J.P. *Patrologiae cursus completus, Series graeca,* 161 vol. Paris-Montrouge, 1857–1866.

———. *Patrologiae cursus completus, Series latina,* 221 vol. Paris-Montrouge, 1844–1864.

Ministry to the Sick (Episcopal). New York: Church Hymnal Corporation, 1977.

Neuner, J. and J. Dupuis (eds.). *The Christian Faith in the Doctrinal Documents of the Catholic Church.* Westminster, Md.: Christian Classics, 1975.

Occasional Services. A Companion to the Lutheran Book of Worship. Minneapolis, Minn.: Augsburg, 1982.

Ordo Unctionis Infirmorum Eorumque Pastoralis Curae. Vatican City: Typis Polyglottis Vaticanis, 1972.

Palmer, Paul F. *Sacraments and Forgiveness.* Sources of Christian Theology, vol. 2. Westminster, Md.: Newman Press, 1959.

Pastoral Care of the Sick: Rites of Anointing and Viaticum. Washington D.C.: ICEL, 1982.

Pastoral Care of the Sick: Rites of Anointing and Viaticum. Ottawa: Canadian Conference of Catholic Bishops, 1983.

The Rites of the Catholic Church. New York: Pueblo, 1976.

Rituale Romanum. Editio prima juxta typicam Vaticanam. New York: Benziger Brothers, 1953.

Santori, G.A. *Rituale sacramentorum romanum.* Rome: 1584.

Theological and Pastoral Orientations on the Catholic Charismatic Renewal. Prepared at Malines, Belgium, May 21–26, 1974. Notre Dame, Ind.: Word of Life, 1974.

Vogel, Cyrille (ed.), *Le Pontificale romano-germanique du dixieme siecle*. (Studi e Testi 226–227). Vatican City: Biblioteca Apostolica Vaticana, 1963.

LITERATURE

Recent Studies In General: Ministry to the Sick, the Aging, and the Dying

Berg, Jan H. van den. *The Psychology of the Sickbed*. Pittsburgh: Duquesne University Press, 1966.

Berrigan, Daniel. *We Die Before We Live. Talking with the Very Ill*.New York: Seabury, 1980.

Borrelli, Susan. *With Care. Reflections of a Minister to the Sick*. Chicago: Liturgy Training Publications, 1980.

Bowman, Leonard. *The Importance of Being Sick: A Christian Reflection*. Wilmington, N.C.: Consortium, 1976.

Bowers, M.K., et al. *Counseling the Dying*. New York: Nelson, 1964.

Clements, William. *Care and Counseling of the Aging*. Philadelphia: Fortress Press, 1979.

"The Coming of Age," *Liturgy* 21:2 (February 1976), special issue.

Deeken, Alfons. *Growing Old and How to Cope with It*. New York: Paulist, 1972.

Dolan, Joseph. *Give Comfort to My People*. New York: Paulist, 1977.

Fournier, William and Sarah O'Malley. *Age and Grace. Handbook of Programs for the Ministry to the Aging*. Collegeville, Minn.: Liturgical Press, 1980.

Hamilton, Michael and Helen Reid (eds.). *A Hospice Handbook. A New Way to Care for the Dying*. Grand Rapids, Mich.: Eerdmann's, 1980.

Kelsey, Morton T. *Prophetic Ministry.* New York: Crossroad, 1982.

"Ministries to the Sick," *Liturgy* 27:2 (1982), special issue.

The Ministry of Healing. Readings in the Catholic Health Care Ministry. St. Louis: The Catholic Health Care Association, 1981.

Niklas, Gerald and Charlotte Stefanics. *Ministry to the Hospitalized.* New York: Paulist Press, 1975.

Nouwen, Henri and Walter Gaffney. *Aging. The Fulfillment of Life.* New York: Doubleday, 1974.

Pastoral Care of the Sick, A Practical Guide for the Catholic Chaplain in Health Care Facilities. Ed. National Association of Catholic Chaplains. Washington, D.C.: USCC, 1974.

Renner, H.P.V. "The Use of Ritual in Pastoral Care," *Journal of Pastoral Care* 33 (1979) 164–174.

"The Sick and the Dying" *Liturgy* 25:2 (1980), special issue.

Studies on the Rites for the Sick and the Dying

Alberton, Mario. *Un sacrement pour les malades.* Paris: Centurion, 1978.

Alszeghy, Zoltan. "The Bodily Effects of Extreme Unction," *Theology Digest* 9 (1961) 105–10.

Béraudy , Roger. "Le sacrement des malades. Etude historique et théologique." *Nouelle Révue Théologique* 96 (1974) 600–34.

Botte, B. "L'onction des malades," *La Maison-Dieu* 15 (1948) 91–107.

Chavasse, A. *Du IIIe siècle à la réforme carolingienne.* Étude sur l'onction des infirmes dans l'église latine du IIe au XIe siecle, vol. 1. Lyons: 1942.

Condon, Kevin. "The Sacrament of Healing (Jas 5:14–16)." In T. Worden (ed.), *Sacraments in Scripture.* Springfield, Ill.: Templegate, 1966, pp. 172–86.

Davis, Charles. "The Sacrament of the Sick or of the Aging," *Theology for Today.* New York: Sheed & Ward, 1962, pp. 248–68.

deClercq, C. "Ordines uncionos infirmides IXe et X^e siécles," *Ephemerides Liturgicae* 44 (1930) 100–122.

Diekmann , Godfrey. "The Laying on of Hands in Healing," *Liturgy* 25 (1980) 7–10, 36–38.

Duval, A. "L'extreme onction au concile de Trente," *La Maison-Dieu* 101 (1970) 127–72.

Empereur, James. *Prophetic Anointing.* Wilmington, Del.: Michael Glazier, 1982.

Glen, M. Jennifer. "Sickness and Symbol: The Promise of the Future," *Worship* 54 (1981) 397–411.

Gusmer, Charles. "Anointing of the Sick in the Church of England, *Worship* 45 (1971), 262–72.

———. "I Was Sick and You Visited Me: The Revised Rites for the Sick," *Worship* 48 (1974) 516–25.

———. "Liturgical Traditions of Christian Illness: Rites of the Sick," *Worship* 46 (1972) 528–43.

Gy, Pierre Marie. "Le nouveau rituel romain de malades," *La Maison-Dieu* 113 (1973) 29–49 (entire issue on anointing).

Isambert, Francois. *Rite et efficacité symbolique. Rites et symboles.* Paris: Cerf, 1979.

Knauber, Adolf. *Pastoral Theology of the Anointing of the Sick.* Collegeville, Minn.: Liturgical Press, 1975.

McLain, J.P. "Anointing of the Sick," *New Catholic Encyclopedia* 1, 568–77.

Marsh, Thomas. "A Theology of Anointing the Sick," *The Furrow* 29 (1978) 89–101.

Mitchell, Nathan. *Cult and Controversy: The Worship of the Eucharist outside Mass.* Studies in the Reformed Rites of the Catholic Church, vol. 4. New York: Pueblo, 1982.

Murray, Placid. "The Liturgical History of Extreme Unction," *Furrow* 11 (1960) 572–93.

Ortemann. *Le sacrement des malades*. Collections "Parole et Tradition." Paris: Chalet, 1971.

Palmer, Paul. "The Purpose of Anointing the Sick: A Reappraisal," *Theological Studies* 19 (1958) 309–44.

———. "Who Can Anoint the Sick?" *Worship* 48 (1974) 81–98.

Porter, H.B. "The Origin of the Medieval Rite for Anointing the Sick or Dying," *Journal of Theological Studies* 7 (1956) 211–25.

———. "Rites for the Dying in the Early Middles Ages," *Journal of Theological Studies* 10 (1959) 43–62, 299–307.

Poschmann, Bernhard. *Penance and the Anointing of the Sick*. New York: Herder, 1963.

Power, David. "Let the Sick Man Call," *The Heythrop Journal* 19:3 (1978), 256–70.

Rites for the Sick and the Dying—National Bulletin on Liturgy 57 (Jan.–Feb. 1977).

Roccariore, Sr. Marie. *Anointing of the Sick and the Elderly*. Canfield, Ohio: Alba, 1980.

Rouillard, Philippe. "Le ministére du sacrement de l'onction des malades," *Nouvelle Revue Théologique* 111:3 (1979) 395–402.

Rush, Alfred. "The Eucharist, The Sacrament of the Dying in Christian Antiquity," *The Jurist* 34 (1974) 10–35.

Sesboüé, Bernard. *L'Onction des Malades*. Lyons: Profac, 1972.

Sicard, Damien. "Le viatique: Perspectives nouvelles?" *La Maison-Dieu* 113 (1973) 103–14.

Spâcil, Theophilus. "Doctrina Theologiae Orientis Separati de Sacra Infirmorum Unctione," *Orientalia Christiana* 24 (1931) 45–259.

Studies on Healing

Cousins, Norman. *Anatomy of an Illness as Perceived by the Patient*. New York: W.W. Norton, 1979.

DiOrio, Ralph A. with Donald Gropman. *The Man Beneath the Gift*. New York: Morrow, 1980.

Faricy, Robert. *Praying for Inner Healing*. New York: Paulist, 1979.

Gusmer, Charles. *The Ministry of Healing in the Church of England: An Ecumenical Liturgical Study*. London: Alcuin Club, 1974.

Kelsey, Morton. *Healing and Christianity*. New York: Harper & Row, 1973.

Linn, Dennis and Matthew Linn. *Healing of Memories. Prayer and Confession—Steps to Inner Healing*. New York: Paulist, 1974.

Linn, Mary Jane, Matthew Linn, and Dennis Linn. *Healing the Dying. Releasing People to Die*. New York: Paulist, 1979.

MacNutt, Francis. *Healing*. Notre Dame, Ind.: Ave Maria Press, 1974.

———. *The Power to Heal*. Notre Dame, Ind.: Ave Maria Press, 1977.

Sanford, John A. *Healing and Wholeness*. New York: Paulist, 1977.

Shlemon, Barbara. *Healing Prayer*. Notre Dame, Ind.: Ave Marie Press, 1976.

Stanley, David. "Salvation and Healing," *The Way* 10 (1970) 298–317.

Talley, Thomas. "Healing: Sacrament or Charism?" *Worship* 46 (1972), 518–27.

Tyrrell, Bernard. *Christotherapy: Healing Through Enlightenment*. New York: Seabury, 1975.

———. *Christotherapy II*. Ramsey, N.J.: Paulist, 1982.

Studies on Dying and Death

Aries, Philippe. *The Hour of Our Death*. New York: Knopf, 1981.

Becker, Ernest. *The Denial of Death*. New York: Free Press, 1973.

Benoit, Pierre and Roland Murphy. *Immortality and Resurrection*. New Concilium Series (Scripture), 1970.

Boros, Ladislaus. *The Mystery of Death*. New York: Herder, 1965.

Cameron, J.M. "On Death and Human Existence," *Worship* 50:3 (1976), 246–60.

Collopy, Bartholomew J. "Theology and Death," *Theological Studies* 39 (March 1978) 22–54.

"En face de la mort," *La Maison-Dieu* 144 (1980), special issue.

Gorer, Geoffrey. *Death, Grief, and Mourning*. Garden City, N.Y.: Doubleday, 1965.

Greinacher, Norbert and Alois Muller. *Death and Dying*. New Concilium Series, 1974.

Kastenbaum, Robert and Ruth Aisenberg. *The Psychology of Death*. New York: Springer, 1972.

Kübler-Ross, Elisabeth. *Death, the Final Stage of Growth*. Englewood Cliffs, N.J.: Prentice-Hall, 1975.

———. *On Death and Dying*. New York: Macmillan, 1969.

———. *Questions and Answers on Death And Dying*. New York: Macmillan, 1974.

———. *Living with Death and Dying*. New York: Macmillan, 1981.

Muckerman, Norman J. (ed.). *How to Face Death without Fear*. Selections from the book *Preparation for Death* by St. Alphonus Liguori. Liguori, Mo.: Liguori Publications, 1976.

Mueller, Mary Louise. "Death Education and Religious Education," *The Living Light*, 12:4 (1975) 562–72.

Rahner, Karl. *On the Theology of Death*. Quaestiones Disputate 2. New York: Herder, 1961.

Rutherford, Richard. *The Death of a Christian: The Rite of*

Funerals, Studies in the Reformed Rites of the Catholic Church, vol. 7. New York: Pueblo, 1980.

Schneidman, Edwin. *Death: Current Perspectives.* New York: Mayfield, 1976.

Steinfels, Peter and Robert Beatch (eds.). *Death Inside Out.* Hastings Center Report. New York: Harper & Row, 1975.

Taylor, Michael (ed.) *The Mystery of Suffering and Death.* New York: Alba, 1973.

Index

and holy communion, 25, 26, 35
in a hospital or institution, 74, 75ff.
by laity, 15, 17, 18, 19, 21, 24, 25, 41, 78, 79, 80
and "last rites," 190
and laying on of hands, 9, 20, 22, 164. *See also separate entry,* Laying
   on of hands
liturgical rite of, 70ff.
Luther on, 33
Lutheran practice of, 39ff.
outside Mass, 70–74
within Mass, 74–75, 160
ministers of, 78–80
with oil, 5–7, 9, 10, 16. *See also separate entry,* Oil
on parts of the body, 23, 24, 32, 68, 69
and paschal mystery, 89
and penance, 26, 27
and prayer, 189
and presbyters, 8–9, 15, 18, 21, 24–25, 41
and priests, 15ff. 19, 32, 33, 41, 78–79
recipient of, 15, 66–67, 78, 82–87
and remission of sins, 10, 16, 20–21, 28, 29, 30–32, 41, 77, 91
revised rite of, 66ff.
as rite for the dying, 30, 31–32
Rituals of, 27–28
as sacrament of the sick, 3, 4, 5, 11, 14f., 19, 30, 66ff., 76–77
as sacramental sign, 67f.
scholastic teaching on, 28ff., 77
and Second Vatican Council, 36, 42
symbolism of, 91
types of, 27f.
on various parts of the body, 68–69, 73
and viaticum, 4, 36, 114. *See also separate entry,* Viaticum

Apostolic Tradition of Hippolytus, 12, 154

Asklepius, 148

Athanasius, 12

Augustine, Saint, 14

Avitus, 18

B

Babylonian Captivity of the Church, 33
Baptism, 79, 84, 115, 160, 164

Frankl, Victor, 144
Freud, Sigmund, 101, 174

G
Gelasian Sacramentary, 13, 67–68, 121
Genevieve, Saint, 18
Glen, Jennifer, 94
Gorer, Geoffrey, 173
Gray Panthers, 174
Gregorian Sacramentary, 13, 67–68

H
Healing
and the paschal mystery, 151–53
as sign of the kingdom, 148–51
Hippolytus, 68
Holy water, blessing and sprinkling with, 26, 123, 126, 161
Hospitals, Christian, 154
Hospitals, and ministry to sick and dying, 183f.
Hugh of St. Victor (d. 1141), 28, 29

I
ICEL, 51, 52, 77
Ignatius of Antioch (d.c. 110), 106
Indulgences, 117
Infant communion, 131
Innocent I, Pope, 14f., 18, 19, 20, 25
International Committee on English in the Liturgy, *see* ICEL
Irenaeus of Lyons (d.c. 202), 146, 156

J
John Chrysostom (d. 407), 110
John of Kronstadt (d. 1908), 156
Jung, C.G., 144
Justin Martyr (d.c. 165), 156